ADVANC|

"Richard draws on his years of experience in the data journey to offer very practical advice for any company serious about becoming data-driven. This is a book you must read if you want to avoid the typical mistakes in this sort of transformation."

DAVID DEL VAL, CEO of Telefónica R&D

"Too many books on AI are pure hype, with no real understanding of its potential and limits, or how to successfully apply it in a business context. *A Data-Driven Company* is the exception: Richard Benjamins has decades of experience in AI technologies and combines this with extensive business experience. He communicates what he has learned with clarity and conviction. This is essential reading for anyone contemplating using AI in large organizations."

MICHAEL WOOLDRIDGE, Professor, University of Oxford and author of *The Road to Conscious Machines*

"If you want to learn how to take the right data-driven decisions in a company that handles big data, you should read this book."

RICARDO BAEZA-YATES, Co-author of the bestseller *Modern Information Retrieval*

Published by
LID Publishing Limited
The Record Hall, Studio 304,
16-16a Baldwins Gardens,
London EC1N 7RJ, UK

info@lidpublishing.com
www.lidpublishing.com

A member of:

businesspublishersroundtable.com

Printed by Severn, Gloucester
ISBN: 978-1-912555-88-8
ISBN: 978-1-911671-31-2 (ebook)

Cover and page design: Caroline Li

**21 LESSONS FOR
LARGE ORGANIZATIONS
TO CREATE VALUE FROM AI**

A DATA-DRIVEN
COMPANY

RICHARD BENJAMINS

MADRID | MEXICO CITY | LONDON
NEW YORK | BUENOS AIRES
BOGOTA | SHANGHAI | NEW DELHI

To my family, for their unconditional support.
Gamy, Hinke, Tina, Indra, Victor, Anke, Mary

To the band, that we keep putting back together.

To Telefónica, for giving me the opportunity to learn.

To all from whom I have learned to be able
to write this book.

Information is not knowledge
Knowledge is not wisdom
Wisdom is not truth

. . ..

FRANK ZAPPA

Truth is not beauty
Beauty is not love
Love is not music
Music is the best

CONTENTS

ACKNOWLEDGEMENTS

Frank Zappa said in his quote: Information is not knowledge, knowledge is not wisdom, wisdom is not truth. A good way to teach others is to share your information, knowledge and wisdom. The truth is hard to share, as nobody can claim to have it.

I would like to thank all data professionals who contributed to this book; thank you very much for your information, knowledge and wisdom:

Thierry Grima[1]

Pedro A. Alonso Baigorri

Pedro A. de Alarcón

Markus Heimann

Marcin Detyniecki

Juan Murillo Arias

Juan Cuenca González

José Luis Agúndez

Jeni Tennison

Jan W Veldsink

Idoia Salazar

Francisco José Montalvo

Eva García San Luis

Elena Gil Lizasoain

Daniel Rodríguez Sierra

Daniel Goberna

Bassey Harrison Umoh

Antonio Pita Lozano

Alberto Turégano Schirmer

I am also grateful to Marcelino Elosua of LID Business Media for his trust in me as an author, and to Aiyana Curtis and Brian Doyle, my editorial manager and copy editor at LID Publishing, for their suggestions and improvements to the manuscript. Finally, I would like to thank Victoria Elosua de Madariaga and serendipity for bringing me to LID.

INTRODUCTION

WHY I WROTE THIS BOOK

Over the course of my career, I have given hundreds of talks at industry events. In the past five years, every time I presented a slide showing 20 decisions that organizations have to face on the journey to become data and AI driven, I noticed strong recognition by the audience. Think of the relation between data and IT, to what function the data department should report, how to measure economic impact, etc. Much has been written about what big data is, how it works, how to apply it to different sectors, what the challenges are, what it means for business, and so on. Yet, there is almost no literature that captures the practical experience of the data and AI transformation, with concrete advice on various options that allow organizations to enjoy the full power of big data and AI while minimizing inappropriate decisions. That made me decide to write this book.

Being a cognitive scientist by training, with specialization in AI, and having always worked in the field of intelligent information systems, big data and AI, I have seen organizations move from viewing data as 'exhaust' from their operation to embracing it as a strategic asset. I've been honoured to be part of this journey in Telefónica for more than ten years, and witnessed it in AXA. Along the way, my participation in more than a hundred big data, analytics and AI events, workshops and conferences through the years has confirmed this need for clear, practical guidance. I learned that about 70% of the data and AI journey is similar across industry sectors, and that 30% is sector-specific. In this book, I will try to capture the 70% that's common to any organization that wants to become data-driven and create value from AI.

WHY DO ORGANIZATIONS WANT TO BECOME DATA-DRIVEN AND AI-POWERED?

A decade ago, a McKinsey report — 'Big data: The next frontier for innovation, competition, and productivity' (Manyika et al., 2011) — brought big data to the attention of corporate boardrooms. Since then, many large enterprises have started their big data journey, as part of their broader digital transformation, to become a data-driven organization. The vision was that big data would help organizations optimize their core business, power new data-driven products and services, and even create entirely new businesses. Today, virtually every business process is run on an IT system, and therefore generates data. This data can be analysed and used for optimizing the process; it can be combined with other data sources to enable further optimization across the enterprise; or, it can be combined with external data sources to help generate even more new opportunities. More recently, the same happened with AI, and AI has overshadowed big data in terms of potential value and attention. Indeed, AI is considered one of today's most promising technologies — it's been compared to revolutionary game changers like electricity and the internet. In fact, many governments have enacted strategies to maximize its benefits, while ensuring that potentially negative side effects are understood and dealt with.

However, becoming data- and AI-driven is not an easy task. It represents a long process that's integral to the digital transformation all large organizations are going through. Figure 0.1 shows Telefónica's data and AI journey, which has been long and complex, with many ups and downs. There are two main learnings from the undertaking:

1. The journey is a phased approach; it's almost impossible to jump directly to the desired end state without going through the previous phases. However, this doesn't mean that phases cannot be partly run in parallel.
2. In order to scale with AI, you first have to become data-driven.

According to a Harvard Business Review article (Bean and Davenport, 2019), "77% of executives report that business adoption of big data/AI initiatives is a major challenge." Fewer than 10% cite technology as a challenge, and the article mentions various other general reasons why becoming data- and AI-driven remains a challenge.

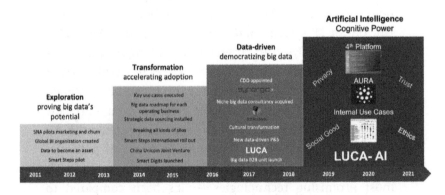

Figure 0.1 The data and AI journey of Telefónica: phases include Exploration, Transformation, Data-driven and AI.

THE BIG DATA
AND AI JOURNEY

The data and AI journey plays a central role in this book because important decision-making depends on the phase of the organization's journey (i.e. its data and AI maturity). At a high level, the journey moves from exploring the opportunity to consolidating the data organization and benefits. The more an organization advances on the journey, the more data can be transformed into value in a scalable manner. In the later phases of the journey, full advantage can be taken of machine learning and AI techniques.

As an illustration, I will discuss the data journey of Telefónica as depicted in Figure 0.1. While each organization's journey will be unique, the main phases, challenges and activities they work through will be more or less similar.

EXPLORATION

The first phase of the data and AI journey is one of exploration. This process can be started bottom-up, by data enthusiasts with technical capability (for instance, some data scientists or data engineers), or top-down, by managers who've heard about the benefits of data for business. Either way, an existing business problem (also known as a 'use case') is typically selected, such as reducing churn or increasing the effectiveness of marketing campaigns. Data is collected, and analytics is applied to see how it solves the problem.

At Telefónica, our exploration phase started in 2011 when we experimented with viral marketing. The objective of the use case was to increase the effectiveness of marketing campaigns for pay TV. Typical campaigns were based on individual customer profiles, and now we wanted to look into the potential of viral campaigns. We used call detail records (CDRs) of the fixed lines and extracted the embedded social graphs (who communicates with whom). Then, we identified groups that were characterized as having many communications, which we interpreted as representing social groups with strong ties. These were usually small groups of between four and six households. We then looked at groups where at least two households already had contracted the pay TV service. The hypothesis was that these two households would have a viral effect on the other members of the group, who would therefore have a higher propensity for buying the service than the average customer. The innovation was that, while customers had only been looked at in isolation, with this new technology their social relationships were also taken into account.

The results of this research were surprising. Looking at all customers included in the campaign, there was not really an effect, positive or negative. However, looking at the new customers resulting from the campaign, it turned out that many belonged to a group that was previously not considered as a segment: households with seniors (age 55-plus). Within this group there was a clear viral effect, and this allowed us to design a specific campaign that ended up driving a high conversion rate.

With these promising results, bringing together data, analytics and business, Telefónica started exploring ways to leverage data at a more global level, across its operations. A global business intelligence (BI) unit was created to get a consolidated view of what was happening in each of the operations, and formulate plans for sharing best practices and lessons learned. I had the honour of running Telefónica's first global BI unit in 2012.

TRANSFORMATION

The objective of the next phase, transformation, was to prepare the organization to treat data as a strategic asset and create value from it in a systematic manner. Activities that were started in this phase included the selection and implementation of strategic use cases, which were deemed to have significant impact on the business. Use case selection happened at the global level, utilizing a kind of 'menu,' with possible options, but implementation was decided locally in each of the operating businesses.

In this phase, we also started a global big data road map to transform the traditional BI practice, which had relied on vendor data warehouses, into a more open big data architecture. At that time, Telefónica selected the Hadoop distribution of Hortonworks as the reference architecture.

Another activity we initiated was the creation of a data sourcing strategy. The telecom sector has a wealth of data available (CDRs, network data, web data, apps data, call centre data, etc.) but collecting and storing it all is not a trivial matter. This data often sits in vendor systems, and it isn't always clear if and under what conditions telecom operators have access to it. Vendors became increasingly aware of the value of data, and in the early days we found that they weren't always willing to provide access to it. An important lesson we learned for contracting with vendors was to always add a clause on data access. With these limitations in mind, Telefónica started to build a data collection road map, progressively adding more data and prioritizing it based on use cases.

Breaking down silos is one of the less-technical challenges that comes with the transformation process. Data sources are always associated with certain business processes, and the business function owner traditionally had control over data generated by the business process. This data owner could decide how to extract key performance indicators (KPIs) from it, and with whom to share subsets of data. When it became clear that data held value, data also became a source of power. Sharing data with other areas of the company was sometimes perceived as losing control and power. With time, however, this resistance weakened, and now all line of business owners see the value of data sharing for the benefit of the organization.

One of the turning points in the transformation phase, and in the data journey itself, was the requirement to make budgeting for big data explicit in the annual strategic plan of all businesses. This made visible what until then was 'hidden' in IT and other budgets. For the first time, it became clear to everybody — from rank and file employees up through middle and senior management — how much each business invested in data and how much value it expected in return. There were many exceptions to the expectation that bigger businesses would invest and harvest more from data. And, this seemingly simple act of making the budget explicit, helped facilitate the requisite culture change. Until then, data professionals had to convince businesses to use data; now businesses were asking data professionals to help them.

When Telefónica started its data journey, the data 'department' was about six reporting steps away from the CEO. By the end of 2019, the Chief Data Officer (CDO) was reporting directly to the CEO. With increasing data maturity, the whole notion of data's strategic importance has slowly progressed up the corporate ladder.

DATA-DRIVEN

Being in the data-driven phase of the journey means that many of the important company decisions are now informed by data — that is, by data-rich insights, in addition to conventional wisdom, experience and intuition. There are, however, still important challenges to overcome.

All companies in this phase have appointed a CDO, or similar executive, who heads a data team. But, what still needs to be achieved is the democratization of this capability, so the benefits aren't only generated by a select group of data professionals, but by every employee in the company. Scaling up the value creation from data is more a cultural issue than a technological one. In this book, we will see how this process can happen.

Another activity that might start in this phase is that companies begin thinking about other ways of deriving value from data. So far, value has been mostly created internally, to improve the business. For some sectors, though, insights generated from first-party data can actually create significant value for other sectors. In Telefónica this is the case for the data that flows through the mobile network. Today, most people have one or two mobile phones, in addition to other devices, connected to the internet. All these devices generate activity in antennas, and this enables the generation of insights from anonymized and aggregated data gleaned from each antenna. Mobile network activity generates footfall and mobility data, which is of great value for sectors such as transportation, tourism, public administration, retail and finance.

Insights from mobile data not only have commercial value, but also social value. In 2016, we set up a dedicated department called Big Data for Social Good (BD4SG) in Telefónica that exploits insights from mobile network data — in combination with open data and other first-party data — to help contribute to achieving the United Nations' Sustainable Development Goals (SDGs). This effort involves close collaboration with humanitarian organizations and other NGOs working on problems such as forced migration, the human toll of natural disasters, child poverty, mobility's impact on climate change and contagious diseases.

ARTIFICIAL INTELLIGENCE

The final phase is where full value can be created from the data, through analytics, machine learning and other AI technologies. This is also where companies might want to reconsider their original data strategy, based on several years of experience and learning, with the aim to scale even more. This may relate to revisiting technological decisions (such as on-premise versus cloud), organizational decisions, or relying on a centralized data team versus a distributed team. It may even extend to creating new business units, while also reconsidering local versus global responsibilities.

In Telefónica, this phase started with applying AI to change the way we interacted with our customers, using so-called 'cognitive computing.' This involved using Natural Language Processing (NLP) technology to automatically understand customer intentions, and then connect these directly to individual customer records to answer customer requests.

In this phase, we also started to view Telefónica as a platform company consisting of four layers. The first platform corresponded to the physical infrastructure (the network, antennas, fibre, shops, etc.). The second layer corresponded to the IT systems to operate the business (so-called OSS and BSS[1] in the telecom industry). The third platform corresponded to the digital services running on top of the other two platforms. The key point is that these first three platforms generate huge amounts of data, and traditionally this data was kept (or not) locally. This is why it always takes so much effort to get decent data needed for use cases: it was dispersed across the company, technically in different physical systems, with different formats and vendors, and owned by different business users. And finally, the fourth platform is a new one that collects all data from the other platforms in an interoperable data format with clear semantics. This fourth platform is now the basis for all of the company's data and AI initiatives.

Making maximum use of big data and AI also brings new risks, particularly related to privacy and the undesired consequences of AI and big data. Putting data and AI at the heart of an organization requires more attention to keeping the data of customers safe, for legal compliance but also to establish and maintain trust. Companies that use data, much of which is generated through how customers interact with company services, have many legal obligations in the European General Data Protection Regulation (GDPR), but also run the risk of reduced customer trust if the data isn't used in a transparent manner. Also, the use of AI throughout the organization requires that companies make sure this technology is always used in a responsible manner. This means avoiding discrimination, putting humans at the centre, and opening black box algorithms when necessary.

Each organization will define or experience its own specific journey to become data-driven and AI-powered. As we said earlier, no two journeys will be alike, but there will be many common themes across them all. This book captures these commonalities such that each organization is able to take informed decisions on the key decision points throughout the journey.

WHAT IS THIS
BOOK ABOUT?

This book will give readers the ability to recognize challenges they face during their digital transformation to become data- and AI-driven, and to address these in terms of decisions to take and alternatives to evaluate and select from. It discusses 21 key decisions that any large organization faces along their journey to become a data-driven and AI company. Large organizations do not always *explicitly* take such decisions, but even if they're unaware of it, they do take these decisions. The lessons are based on experience over an intense ten years of activity in two large organizations, and on conversations with many others at more than a hundred industry events. It's surprising to see how similar the challenges are across different industry sectors. This book captures these common challenges.

Most chapters include an external perspective from an experienced data professional — we spoke with experts from a range of different companies and sectors. The goal has been to enrich the lessons learned with real-world experiences and specific conclusions.

This book is not about technical aspects of data science and big data architecture, nor is it about explaining data science or AI to business people. It is about how to progress on the digital transformation journey, of which data and AI are key ingredients. At the same time, the book is not an exhaustive checklist of what to consider on the journey. It is, rather, a lessons-learned approach that spotlights the main decision points that companies face.

WHO SHOULD READ THIS BOOK?

This book is aimed at data professionals with an interest in their organization becoming more data- and AI-literate, and who want to take full advantage of the possibilities offered by these powerful technologies. It adds value for both organizations that want to start, as well as those who are already in the process but want to move to the next phase. Typical professionals who can learn from this book include:

- New and established Chief Data, Chief AI or Chief Analytics Officers responsible for leading their organization to becoming data-driven.
- Data scientists, AI engineers and other data professionals with an interest in progressing toward a CDO role.
- CEOs who want to understand what they can expect if they decide to become a data-driven or AI-powered organization (business aspects, investments, challenges).
- CFOs who need to know how to fund the data journey and what returns to expect.
- Anyone with an interest in understanding how companies (slowly) move forward on their data and AI digital transformation.

WHAT WILL YOU LEARN?

By the end of this book you will understand:
- That there are different stages of the data journey, and what their characteristics are.
- What kind of organizational, technological, business, people and ethical decisions any organization needs to think about when wanting to become more data-driven and AI-powered.
- The different options available when taking a decision to move forward with this transformation.
- The pros and cons of the various options available, and what alternatives are best in certain circumstances.
- Practical examples of options available and decisions taken.
- The actual experiences of 20 data professionals who are, to some extent, driving the data transformation in their organizations.

THE STRUCTURE OF THE BOOK

The book is structured in different parts, each grouping the relevant decisions related to a specific aspect of the journey and looking at the journey from different perspectives.

PART I – Organization is about decisions related to organizational aspects of becoming data- and AI-driven. This includes decisions such as:
- Where to place the Chief Data Officer on the organizational chart.
- How data and IT live together.
- Whether to position AI in the data organization or elsewhere.
- How to measure data maturity.
- External monetization of data.

PART II – Business and finance discusses the main business decisions related to data and AI, including:
- How to select AI and big data use cases.
- How to measure economic impact.
- How to fund the data and AI journey.
- How to approach open data.
- Implementation of AI and big data in small- and medium-sized enterprises.

PART III – Technology is about the tech decisions that organizations will face during their data and AI journey, including questions relating to:
- Cloud versus on-premise hosting.
- Relying on local or global data storage, and whether to adopt a unified data model.
- Where to run the analytics (globally or locally).
- Data collection strategy.
- Working with external providers and partners.

PART IV – *People* discusses people-related considerations, such as:
* Winning over sceptics.
* Data democratization; scaling insights throughout the company.
* How to market the results and create momentum with data.

PART V – *Responsibility* is about the social and ethical implications of using AI and big data, including:
* The social and ethical challenges of AI and big data.
* The importance of AI principles and the responsible use of AI.
* Using big data and AI for 'good.'

PART I

ORGANIZATION

In this first section, we discuss the decisions that are related to organizational aspects of the data and AI journey. These decisions address:

- Where to put the data and AI department on the organizational chart.
- How to articulate the relationship with IT.
- Whether to combine data and AI or analytics.
- How to measure data maturity.
- Whether external monetization requires a separate organization.

1. WHERE SHOULD THE CHIEF DATA OFFICER BE PLACED ON THE ORGANIZATIONAL CHART?

With big data and AI becoming such a big deal in the world of business, it's no surprise that the Chief Data Officer (CDO) has gained a seat at the boardroom table.

The first CDO was appointed in 2002 by Capital One (Davenport and Randy, 2020), and over the past few years an increasing number of organizations — mostly in the private sector, but also publicly-owned businesses — have come to see data as a strategic asset and have appointed CDOs. One survey (NewVantage Partners, 2021) found that 65% of firms reported having appointed a CDO in 2021, up from just 55.6% in 2018.

Until the appearance of this new role, business intelligence (BI) and big data initiatives had often been dispersed throughout organizations, working in isolated departments, even if there was supposedly a central BI team keeping tabs on the overall company BI strategy. With the rise of the strategic importance of data, many organizations will want to appoint a CDO as the central responsible figure for their data strategy and execution. Typical questions that organizations face when appointing a CDO include:

- How far should the CDO be from the CEO? CEO-1[1] or CEO-2, CEO-n?
- If it is CEO-1, how does the CDO relate to the other corporate officers, in particular the CIO and CTO?

- If it is CEO-n, to which executive should the CDO report? Should it be the Chief Information Officer (CIO), Chief Operating Officer (COO), Chief Marketing Officer (CMO), Chief Financial Officer (CFO), Chief Transformation Officer, Chief Technology Officer or Chief Digital Officer?

HOW CLOSE SHOULD THE CDO BE TO THE CEO?

To leverage the full potential of data, the CDO is best placed in an area whose mission is cross-company, representing a large chunk of the business. In this way, the value creation is not limited to one specific area (e.g. marketing), and the value is relevant for the business. Doing otherwise creates a bias toward creating value only from data in a specific area, or in an area that is not directly focused on business.

Therefore, many argue that the best place to position the CDO is at CEO-1 or at CEO-2 — specifically, under the COO, giving the executive cross-company responsibility. Having the CDO report directly to the CEO gets him or her a seat on the Executive Committee, which delivers a strong message both internally and externally. There are two alternative senior executives who also ensure cross-organizational application and relevance: the Chief Transformation Officer and the Chief Digital Officer. While these two roles are temporary in nature (albeit active for many years), they work in a cross-organizational manner and are tasked with the mission of adapting their business to the digital world, of which data is a pivotal part.

Of course, having the CDO report directly to the CEO isn't necessarily suitable for all organizations at all times. It requires a level of data maturity, and is likely to be reserved for the more forward-looking organizations that really know and embrace the fact that they have to adapt to the digital world in a data-driven way.

So, why would organizations not (yet) want a CEO-1 position for the CDO?

- Some companies may be too immature from a data perspective, and therefore might want to place the CDO under the CIO, within the IT function. This would help ensure that there's sufficient technological understanding before starting to use data for business.

- Some organizations have a very clear idea of where to start exploiting data, so they place the CDO under the corresponding department. For example, companies in sectors such as fast-moving consumer goods (FMCG) — with a strong interest in improving their consumer marketing — might put the CDO under the CMO. Those who want to innovate with data might even place the CDO under the CTO (R&D), while organizations that want to save money might position him or her under the Global Resources Officer.

WHERE TO LOCATE THE CDO AREA?

In general, if the CDO is placed within a specific area, this implies that the executive inherits some of the objectives of that area. If situated under marketing, then objectives will probably be oriented toward sales or revenue. If under Global Resources, the executive's goals will likely be related to savings. Helping areas outside of their specific area then becomes a 'best effort' thing, rather than a core responsibility, depending on the CDO's bandwidth and how collaborative he or she is. However, experience teaches us that it is challenging to see this kind of cooperation beyond the day-to-day corporate limits of KPIs.

So, if an organization decides to place the CDO under one of the CEO-1 executives, without cross-organizational responsibility, it creates an unnecessary limitation to value creation from data. But why, then, are most CDOs not CEO-1, but -2 or sometimes even CEO-3 or -4? Table 1.1 lists the pros and cons that influence why an organization might do it this way:

Area	Pros	Cons
CMO	Marketing and sales provide use cases with direct impact	Usually focused on B2C, forgetting the B2B area, not capturing value in other areas
CFO	Financial ledger requires high-quality data	Less business focused, and financial management doesn't need big data
CIO	Technology used according to company standards	Governed by technological criteria, not business
CTO	Take advantage of the latest technological innovations	Driven by new technology, rather than by business
CSO (security)	Good for security and privacy of customer data	Less focus on business
CRO (resources)	Cost savings go directly to the bottom line	Driven by efficiency, rather than growth

Table 1.1 The pros and cons of a CDO's position in the organizational chart

Organizations that have decided to become data driven as an important part of their digital transformation usually appoint a CDO at CEO-2 level. At this point, it is important to reflect on where to locate the CDO area, and to take an explicit decision based on some of the learnings explained in this chapter. When the organization's data maturity increases, the CDO might become CEO-1, but that's not regularly happening.

Of course, whether a CDO is successful depends not only on where the role resides in the organization, but that remains an important factor. You can explore other relevant considerations in the work of strategic data management consultant Jay Zaidi (Zaidi, 2015), such as business sponsorship or a lack of clarity on the role.

At Telefónica, the CDO function was introduced to the Executive Committee at the end of 2015, and since then has been held by three different individuals. Ten years ago, the data areas were scattered around the company, with the responsible executives positioned between CEO-5 and -6. Seven years ago, it became -4, and six years ago it rose to CEO-2. In 2015 it was elevated to CEO-1 on the organizational chart, showing just how fundamental data had become in Telefónica's digital transformation strategy.

The discussion of where to place the CDO, and at what level, is quite relevant for those organizations on the journey to becoming data driven. However, among 'native data' companies, whose business *is* the data, the CDO has very different requirements. A Gartner report on the four types of CDO organizations (Gartner, 2016) noted that the CDO is even more critical in data companies. One could argue that it makes sense in such companies for this executive to actually be the CEO. We may not know what the future holds for big corporations, but we do know that it will be driven by data.

CONCLUSION

The CDO is the champion of the data and AI journey. As such, the role — similar to that of a Chief Transformation Officer or Chief Digital Officer — is temporal in nature. When the journey is completed, data has the status of a strategic asset and will be managed accordingly. While one of the key responsibilities of the CDO at the beginning of the journey was to serve as a change agent, in data-driven companies, managing data and creating value from it across the organization is now business as usual (BAU). This might result in somewhat lower-profile (but definitely not less important) CDOs in data-mature organizations.

While this could be interpreted, somewhat dramatically, as 'the rise and fall of Chief Data Officers,' in reality it is the logical way of dealing with disruptive organizational changes. CDOs will not disappear, but the nature of the position is inherently evolutionary. In the beginning, they may be held responsible for anything related to data and corresponding value creation, while in mature, data-driven companies their role will be focused on the data management side: to curate a strategic asset. Value creation from that asset is now allocated to the appropriate departments throughout the organization, allowing for maximum scale of benefit creation.

COMMON ERRORS IN THE JOURNEY TO BECOME DATA DRIVEN

PEDRO A. ALONSO BAIGORRI

Telecommunications Engineer, Global Data Product Manager at Telefónica Tech

In the last ten years I have been lucky enough to participate in the digital transformation of a leading technology company into a data-driven enterprise. During this time, we have taken on projects and initiatives of all kinds, most of which have been successful and have undoubtedly allowed us to move closer to the goal of data conversion as the main source of decision-making and value generation. However, along the way, mistakes have inevitably been made that have somewhat slowed down this process. I'd like to highlight the ones that I consider the most important, which can serve as learning for other, similar initiatives in the future:

1. **Being blinded by technology:** The new big data and AI technologies are highly attractive, especially for the most technologically minded people. When a data-driven project begins, they will inevitably be attracted to it, and the first thing to think about is which big data platform to build or which AI algorithm to use — the more sophisticated the better. However, this is like building a house from the roof on down. To begin with, it is essential to be clear about the business problems that need to be solved, to identify what relevant data you have to call upon, and to ensure that the data is of sufficiently high quality. Once your data is in order, you can start analysing it to solve your business problem. Note that the latest technology is not always essential to accomplish this. Sometimes a simple Excel spreadsheet or an SQL database is enough to start. Further

down the line, when the amount of data is a lot bigger and the problems are more complex, big data and AI technologies will certainly help, and they'll be of vital importance when it comes to getting the most out of the data.

2. **Not protecting your data in the services provided by external platforms:** Nowadays, there are more and more digital services provided by external platforms hosted in the cloud (e-commerce tools, financial services, logistics, etc.). A recurring mistake when executing commercial agreements with these providers is to forget to include clauses ensuring that data generated by the services belongs to the client company, and that the supplier will provide it through APIs or similar mechanisms so the data can be used internally. Without such contractual agreement, it can be extremely difficult to later access the data and have permission to use it. Do not leave questions of data ownership open to interpretation.

3. **Concentrating insight generation in a single depart-ment:** It is also a common mistake to anoint centres of expertise — for instance, in BI or big data functions — as the sole parties responsible for analysing the company's data and obtaining business insights. These areas usually have experts in data analysis, but without a business context it is impossible to gain relevant insights. Insight generation has to be a process that's totally transversal to the company. That is, it must intersect and be intermeshed with the various lines of business. Any area — whether it is business, HR, product marketing, etc. — must have the tools and the knowledge to access the data, analyse it and reach conclusions that allow the best decisions to be made at all times. Obviously, BI and big data experts must support the initiative with their greater knowledge of data analysis technology and algorithms, but it must be a joint effort.

For this to happen, it makes sense to position big data and AI experts within a company's business areas, to facilitate this collaborative work and help change the organizational culture.

4. **Overuse of black box algorithms:** Another frequent mistake is to blindly trust the results of so-called black box algorithms – systems that are so complex that their inner workings cannot be observed or easily interpreted, even by data scientists who design them. Thanks to mathematics, these offer a quick way to detect customers who are potentially going to abandon the brand (churners) or those with a propensity to buy a product or service. However, on many occasions, it is essential not only to know the result of the algorithm, but also how it works. In the case of churners, it's not only necessary to know who's most likely to take their business elsewhere, but also the reasons why. With greater insight into that reasoning, the organization acquires greater confidence when making decisions based on data, and it can make more concrete decisions on how to act on the result of the algorithm. For the customer with a probability of taking their business elsewhere, you will be able to know what you should do to retain them. For example, in the telecom space, it's important to know whether it's due to them having an outdated mobile, a service plan that's not appropriate to their needs, or technical problems with the line.

Turning a business into a data-driven operation is a long and complex journey, especially for large corporations. As mentioned, mistakes will inevitably be made, but the important thing is to learn from them. Of course, it is much better and more efficient to be aware of the mistakes made by others before you make them yourself.

2. DATA AND IT – HOW DO THEY LIVE TOGETHER?

Many things related to data are about information technology (IT). Systems, platforms, development, operations and security are all needed for creating value from data, and are traditionally in the realm of IT. Yet, data implies specific technologies requiring particular profiles and skills. It's therefore no wonder that many organizations struggle with where to position these responsibilities. In the previous chapter, we discussed several approaches to where a business might 'host' its CDO. The conclusion was that the executive is best situated where he or she is transversal to the business and matters to the business — for example, under the Chief Operating Officer, Chief Transformation Officer or Chief Digital Officer. While this is an important organizational decision, wherever the CDO sits, he or she will always need to collaborate extensively with IT (usually the CIO). But, what is the best relationship between data, on the one hand, and IT on the other?

PROS AND CONS OF ALTERNATIVE ORGANIZATIONS FOR DATA AND IT

Let's examine the different options for organizing data and IT in an organization. As we'll see, there are various alternatives, each with its advantages and disadvantages.

Organizations in a 'green field' position — building their strategy and organization from the ground up — have a chance to weigh all options for their specific situation and then choose the best approach. However, many organizations will already have some structures in place, and may not be able to choose the best options, but will still be able to explicitly choose a second-best approach.

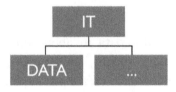

Figure 2.1 Data reports to IT, reflecting the large technological component of data

In Figure 2.1, data is reporting to IT, reflecting its strong technological foundations. While this might be a good option at the beginning of the data journey, because it's impossible to start data without technology, it lacks business as the driver of data. For this reason, many organizations that have already started their data journey are not using this structure today. They recognize that the value of data must be driven by business needs.

Figure 2.2 Data and IT are independent departments, reporting into different parts of the organization

Figure 2.2 illustrates a different approach, where the data and IT departments report into independent parts of the organization. For instance, data might report into the marketing area, whereas IT sits under the CIO. In such organizations, the relationship is usually a client-provider dynamic. This organizational structure usually causes problems. For example, data is still a relatively new area and therefore needs many interactions with IT (install new software/libraries, modify permissions, install updates, etc.). Client-provider organizations function through a demand-management system with contractual service level agreements (SLAs), and while that may be sufficient for commodity IT programs, for rapidly evolving technology this does not work when simple things may take weeks to complete. For this reason, Gartner introduced the Bimodel approach for IT (Altimetrik, 2015). Moreover, with this decoupled structure, unresolved conflicts between data and IT require a complex escalation process, sometimes all the way up to the Executive Committee. That creates an enormous obstacle for the agility that's so necessary when setting up new data departments.

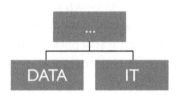

Figure 2.3 Data and IT are reporting to a common 'boss'

In Figure 2.3, data and IT are both directly reporting to the same manager. The benefit of this organizational structure is alignment and coordination by design, and in case there are problems, escalation is simple, setting the stage for quick resolution. Organizations that aren't constrained by legacy decisions and structures (green field operations) might opt for this approach.

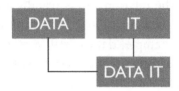

Figure 2.4 Data and IT report into different organizations, but IT has a specific area dedicated to data, possibly with a dotted reporting line to data

In Figure 2.4, data and IT are both reporting somewhere in the organization, but IT has fenced off a dedicated group of people to focus on data. To reinforce this focus, a dotted reporting line to data can be introduced. There are several advantages to this structure:

- The data area will be better served by IT because, under normal circumstances, it doesn't have to compete with other IT priorities.
- It ensures alignment between the technology that data is using and the strategic choice of IT.
- The data IT people are still part of the larger IT organization, allowing for training, rotating to other interesting IT projects, etc.

The disadvantages relate to the fact that sometimes the standard, approved IT technology might not be suitable for rapidly changing technology in the data space. Moreover, there are challenges with the teams. Do the data IT people have data or IT objectives? Or, are they responsible for a mix of both? What happens when the larger IT organization is under pressure? Will it still respect the data priorities, while not necessarily seeing this effort reflected in its wider objectives? People in the data IT team might also feel they have two bosses: their data boss, determining their daily work priorities, and their 'administrative' IT boss, who decides their bonus. If IT and data get along well, there should be no issue. Unfortunately, in practice that isn't always the case. One of the key factors in making this structure work is co-location of the data and data IT teams. While this doesn't solve the HR problems, it does create a sense of belonging to one team, which helps smooth over the aforementioned challenges.

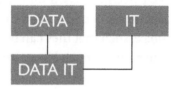

Figure 2.5 Data and IT report into different organizations, but data has its own
IT area, possibly with a dotted reporting line to IT

Figure 2.5 illustrates a construct where data and IT still report into different organizational units (as in Figure 2.4), but now the data team has its own IT department, possibly with a dotted reporting line to IT. This structure has the same advantages of the previous model, and additionally solves some of the challenges of the positioning in Figure 2.4. Notably, for the data IT team it is now crystal clear who their boss is and who decides on their bonus. The disadvantage is the risk of a disconnect between technology used for data versus the official IT tech standard. Moreover, it becomes harder for data IT people to rotate to other interesting IT projects, since they aren't formally part of the IT organization. The dotted line will rectify these issues to some extent, but they still need to be managed carefully.

CONCLUSION

There are many ways to organize the dependency, inter-action and collaboration between the data area and the IT area. While there are some recognized best practices (and undeniably 'bad' practices), there is no one best solution that works for all organizations. They're all different, many already have existing structures in place, and they're simply not free to take any decision they would like, even if it would clearly be the best option. A good practice is to evaluate the different alternatives, as explained in this chapter, and take an explicit decision based on the pros and cons. One of the key learnings is to understand the disadvantages of the eventual choice, such that they can be explicitly managed before they turn into a much bigger problem.

THE CORRECT MANAGEMENT OF MULTIDISCIPLINARY TEAMS AS A KEY TO THE SUCCESS OF DATA AND ANALYTICAL PROJECTS

JUAN CUENCA GONZÁLEZ
Chief Data Officer,
Equifax Iberia

Addressing a data and analytical project is comparable to shooting a film in which there are a multitude of roles that must be perfectly coordinated with each other to produce a harmonious result. Therefore, one of the key factors in ensuring the success of these projects is knowing how to properly manage their complexity and governance. This is never an easy task, due to the number of different disciplines and areas that need to be involved (business knowledge, algorithms and mathematics, technological architecture and software engineering, processes, legal, etc).

Following this approach, such projects cannot be driven from a single function or area of the company. It is advisable to involve at least one business unit, as well as the data and analytics (D&A) and IT areas. Depending on the scope and complexity of the project, the involvement of multiple functional areas — legal, process, channels, etc. — will also be required. In this sense, it's important to ensure that such different and complementary areas, which need each other, work closely together. Indeed, a common mistake is to use the classic customer-supplier relationship models for these projects. Experience shows that this methodology tends to consolidate the silos and borders between the functional areas, preventing the close integration of disciplines required to guarantee optimum project results.

Consequently, some keys to achieving success and adding value are based on joint, well-coordinated work between all the 'actors in this film.' It's therefore advisable to set up multidisciplinary project teams that include representatives from all areas, aligned by a common business objective. In these teams, mixed expertise profiles — with knowledge of several functional competencies at the same time — are especially valuable. They tend to glue together areas that usually speak different languages and don't often understand each other well.

On the other hand, it is important to define clear processes for project governance, in which all areas are involved from the very beginning, although each plays a different role in each phase of the project and leadership is transferred between them in the different stages.

And, of course, when it comes to data and analytics, it is also advisable to establish results- and metrics-monitoring systems for the project, with shared and visible indicators for all team members and their managers, so that the team's performance and effectiveness can be monitored.

3. IS AI INCLUDED IN THE DATA ORGANIZATION OR IS IT SEPARATE?

In the previous chapter, we saw how data and IT are related and how they can be organized. In this chapter, we will see that data is closely related to adjacent areas, and discuss what the different organizational options are.

Big data entered business organizations at large scale beginning in 2011, when McKinsey Global Institute wrote the seminal report, 'Big data: The next frontier for innovation, competition, and productivity' (Manyika et al., 2011). A similar report about analytics that runs on top of big data was published by McKinsey in 2017 (Henke et al., 2016), and the think tank's third report, also in 2017, examined the impact of AI (Bughin et al., 2017). This phased business-readiness of these technologies is today reflected in how organizations set up related areas.

The first new role and corresponding department that found its way into corporations was the CDO, whose main responsibility was a mixture of setting up big data platforms and performing some kind of analytics on the data, for delivering insights and use cases. A few years later, the role of the Chief Analytics Officer (CAO) was introduced, and there were even hybrid Chief Data and Analytics Officer (CDAO) appointments. With the rise of AI, there are now also plenty of Chief AI Officers (CAIOs).

Many organizations that have embarked on their data and AI journey, as well as those that are about to start, wonder how to organize all these different departments and what their relationships and reporting lines should be. Depending on whether they're starting from scratch or already on the journey, the decision may be different. However, the underlying concepts and principles remain the same, and are explained in this chapter.

CONSIDERATIONS FOR ORGANIZING DATA, ANALYTICS AND AI-RELATED AREAS

First of all, data is the basis for analytics and is fuelling many AI applications. Indeed, the dominant AI paradigm in business today is data-driven AI, also known as machine learning. Machine learning takes as input large amounts of historical data and generates a program or model that's able to make predictions on what will happen, for instance, or perform a classification based on new data that the model has never seen before. It might be used to determine which customers will switch to the competition, what components will break down in an industrial plant, what movie to recommend, or whether a particular patient is suffering from a certain disease. Machine learning is therefore dependent on the availability of quality data.

AI is broader than just machine learning. There is NLP, Knowledge Representation & Reasoning, Planning and Robotics. And while several of these areas have enjoyed breakthroughs in the past few years thanks to machine learning, they aren't only about machine learning.

For the machine learning type of AI, it's important that the AI department is not too far from the data department (the CDO), especially at the start of the data journey, when frequent interactions are necessary. In this sense, the same principles behind the choices for data and IT discussed in the previous chapter also apply to how to organize data, analytics and AI. That means that these three areas should report into the same senior executive, and preferably have the same direct manager. The reason is simple: if there are issues between the different areas, the escalation process is straightforward and fast, speeding up resolution. Conversely, having the data, analytics and AI in organizations that report to different senior executives is a recipe for problems and even failure. Different senior execs likely have different tangible objectives, and what might be essential for the CMO might be less relevant for the CIO at a particular time. That might put differing emphasis on the priorities of one team or the other, and they may be out of sync. Solving such a problem requires escalating it all the way up to the board, which takes time and effort, generates frustration and delays progress on the digital transformation.

Of course, if the focus of an AI organization is not on machine learning, but on the other, non-data intensive areas, it doesn't hurt to have it in a separate organization, as there is less dependency. As soon as data starts becoming the main driver, though, they should be put together.

Another reason these three areas (data, analytics, AI) should be close together is that these technologies are still relatively new in the business world, and organizations lack experience in how they can work together. As such, mistakes may be made in each distinct area, requiring backtracking on earlier decisions; this backtracking has an impact on what was communicated earlier to the other areas.

THE RELATION WITH
DATA MATURITY

As we will see, for many decisions, the data maturity of an organization is an important factor in making the best decision. In other words, depending on how data-mature an organization is, how a particular decision is made is less or more relevant. For relatively immature organizations — those that have recently started this journey — it's crucial to have the AI and data departments close together, as we have argued here. However, for more mature organizations with significant experience, this is less of an issue. Data-mature organizations have data management and governance in place, ensuring a certain quality and frequency of the data. If the data is good, AI and analytics areas can work on their own. In more data-immature organizations, data availability and quality are not well-organized processes, and much faster, more agile interactions are needed to obtain results.

DO YOU NEED DATA SCIENTISTS
OR DATA ENGINEERS?

The rise of big data has been accompanied by the ascent of the data scientist, which has been called the sexiest job of the 21st century (Davenport and Patil, 2012). This motivated many data professionals to profile themselves as data scientists, and has led to the hiring of an abundance of data scientists by organizations looking to strengthen their data team. In reality, however, the majority of effort in a data project is dedicated to accessing and understanding the data and verifying its quality, with a much smaller part dedicated to the analytics or machine learning.

This is a logical consequence of the overall low data maturity of organizations in the past few years. Only when data is fully managed as an asset can full attention be devoted to value creation with analytics and machine learning. But today, such organizations (mostly big tech companies) represent only a small percentage. This trend has led to many professionals hired as data scientists working at accessing and manipulating data for the sake of data, rather than creating value, and this has led to much frustration.

The lesson learned here is that, in practice, organizations need to hire the right balance of data engineers and data scientists. At the beginning of the data journey, there should be more data engineers than data scientists, and with increasing data maturity the balance can shift in favour of the data scientists ... but not earlier!

This phenomenon also has important implications for groups within the different data departments. For organizations starting their data and AI journey, it would be a mistake to separate the data and analytics/AI areas. The data department would do its best to collect, store, organize and make data available, but given the early stage, this process will likely take a long time and generate doubtful data quality. This leads to frustration in the analytics/AI team: they're waiting for data, and once it is there, it has a lot of problems and they need to refer back to the data department. The further away the departments are in the organizational structure, the more frustration there will be, which will negatively impact the collaboration. As discussed in the previous chapter, the optimal positioning is to have the departments report to the same line manager. If this isn't possible, one of the alternate solutions we suggested may make sense, such as co-location or dotted line reporting.

CONCLUSION

How to organize the respective data departments (data, analytics and AI) depends on where the organization is on its data journey. Especially in early phases, it is important to keep them as close together as possible. Fully data-mature organizations have more flexibility in where to put the different teams, as data will be part of the BAU processes. It's always better to view the association between the different departments as 'partner' and not 'client-provider' relationships.

SHOULD AI AND BIG DATA BE
PART OF THE SAME DEPARTMENT?

**EVA GARCÍA
SAN LUIS**
KPMG Partner, Head
of KPMG Lighthouse,
CoE Analytics, AI,
Emerging Technologies

If you were to ask this question five years ago, it would have had to be rephrased as, 'Should machine learning and big data be part of the same department?' That's because at that time only a few were concerned about AI. And, in many cases, the answer would have been, 'Aren't they the same?'

They are not, of course! Machine learning and AI deal with mathematical models to generalize patterns from a data set. Big data makes big data sets available to the right people in the right moment (which usually means immediately), not only for AI but for any area in the company that performs some kind of data analysis.

Why, then, should they be in the same department? The skills, in principle, are totally different: mathematicians versus experts in data architecture. The classic solution to provide big data inside the company has been to develop so-called data lakes. The data lake holds all the information that data scientists and AI practitioners would need for their work. They don't have to worry about the details of data processing. The data is curated, formatted, protected and available under the big data 'stuff' for high-speed processing: Hadoop, Spark, NoSql — you probably already know this list. This organizational model has been implemented in many companies and is considered a best practice.

Now, let's imagine an AI project in a large bank whose goal is to analyse all legal documents and extract important clauses that require a follow-up. This kind of data probably hasn't been uploaded to the data lake yet. In that case, we need to go to the big data department and explain the project, the data sources and how we are going to access the data. We then need to interact with the big data guys again during the typical project phases: data exploration, data preprocessing, training and execution. They will have to adapt the initial architecture to allow efficient text processing of tens of thousands of contracts. And, everything is for this single project.

AI projects usually have two entangled features that make them difficult to integrate in a corporate data lake: novelty and creativity. New problems will need new forms of data not initially anticipated in the data lake. Creativity is killed if the AI engineer has to go through a lot of administrative steps to perform a job that is basically scientific research with a lot of trial and error. Data lakes are a very good solution for well-defined problems that have already been solved — and they represent a good practice that should not be abandoned — but this isn't the best platform for innovative AI projects.

A compromise is to make a self-service cloud-like infrastructure available to the AI people so they can upload and process the data on their own. In the AI team we should have people with strong skills in both AI and data architecture, which are not so rare because they face these kinds of problems often. On the other hand, they should be subjected to certain rules. For instance, bank contracts can't go to an external cloud, and they have to be defined in advance to preserve confidentiality. And finally, there must be a clear procedure to efficiently move the result to the production environment.

This is similar to what many R&D departments do in the industry: they can often use small production facilities to develop and test new products without disturbing the real production process. Only when the new product is ready are the production facilities adapted to test and host it.

4. **HOW TO MEASURE YOUR DATA MATURITY**

As we've seen, many organizations have started their journey to become more data-driven and better positioned to take automated, intelligent decisions. But, this journey is a complex process, with several intermediate stages. While it is relatively clear what the stages are and what kind of activities they comprise (illustrated in Figure 4.1), it is less clear how to assess the overall data maturity of an organization with respect to its goal to fuel analytics and AI.

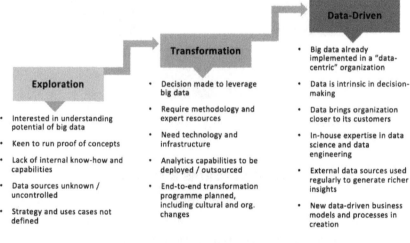

Figure 4.1 The phases of a typical data journey toward becoming a data-driven organization

DIMENSIONS OF DATA MATURITY

Indeed, measuring the data maturity of organizations is a multidimensional activity, covering a wide range of areas. In this chapter, we will provide an overview of these dimensions and how to measure progress on each of them. Figure 4.2 shows the dimensions, which we explain below using examples of what it means to be less or more mature.

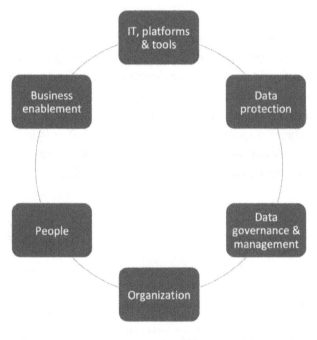

Figure 4.2 The dimensions of measuring organizational data maturity

IT, PLATFORMS & TOOLS

Any organization that wants to do something with data and AI needs a platform where data is stored and accessed. Early-stage, immature organizations won't likely have any platform to start with, either in the cloud or on-premise, and no particular strategy. Conversely, mature organizations will have a clear strategy for how to support all facets of data needed for analytics and AI. The strategy will encompass whether systems will run on-premise, in the cloud or using a hybrid approach. It will describe the reference architecture for the big data software stack, APIs for accessing data in secure ways, etc. It will also cover the analytics, data visualization and data quality tools available for users across the organization. Mature organizations will have automated most of the processes to run the platforms and tools on a daily basis, with minimum manual intervention. Finally, mature companies have a clear budget assigned to this, along with a data road map of new functionalities and new data sources to include.

DATA PROTECTION

Data protection refers to ensuring the privacy and security of the organization's data. It can also be viewed as part of data governance, but due to its importance it's often considered separately. Thanks to the GDPR, it is clear for many organizations what it means to protect privacy of personal customer data. However, for most it's still a major challenge to comply with all aspects of the GDPR. Because the regulation has set the bar high, we can say that those that are fully GDPR compliant are mature on the data protection front. In addition, data-mature organizations use all kinds of privacy-enhancing technologies, such as encryption, anonymization & pseudonymization, and differential privacy, to reduce the risk of revealing personal information. With respect to security, apart from the technological solutions for secure data storage, transfer, access and publishing, mature organizations also have a clear policy on who has access to what types of data, with special attention given to those with administrator rights who might be able to access all data, encryption and hashing keys.

DATA GOVERNANCE & MANAGEMENT

This dimension measures how well data is managed as an asset. Almost all organizations that started their data journey some time ago will recognize that some of the biggest problems are associated with accessing quality data, understanding what all data fields mean, and understanding the provenance (data lineage). Managing data as an asset includes things like having an up-to-date inventory of all data sources, a data dictionary, and a master data-management solution with data quality and lineage. But, it is also about processes, ownership and stewardship. Data sources typically have an owner who's responsible for the data generation, either as a consequence of an operation — perhaps payment data generated by point-of-sale (POS) devices — or through explicit data collection. A data steward takes care of the data on a daily basis, in terms of availability, quality, updates, etc. Organizations that take data seriously tend to set up a 'data management office' that functions as a centre of excellence to advise the different stakeholders in the organization. More advanced organizations not only manage their data, but also their analytical models throughout their lifecycle. They will also consider external data, either procured or as open data, to increase the value potential. At the same time, the most mature organizations have a clear policy on open data, stating how it should be managed (license, liability, updates, etc.), as well as when and under what circumstances privately-held data can be published as open data, and under what license (see Chapter 9).

ORGANIZATION

The organization dimension refers to how the data professionals are organized in the company. Is there a separate organization, like a Chief Data Officer? How powerful is this position in terms of distance from the CEO (-1, -2, -3)?

Or, are the data professionals split between several organizations, such as IT, Marketing and Finance? What is the function of the data team? Is it a centre of excellence or is it operational, running all data operations of the company on a daily basis? Also, how well are the data professionals connected to the different lines of business? Is there a company-wide 'data board,' where data leaders and business leaders share, discuss and take decisions to align business and data priorities? Is there an initiative to democratize the data, extending availability beyond the data professionals to the business people? And then, how is the next layer of people involved in creating value from data (see Chapter 17)?

PEOPLE

The people dimension is all about how organizations acquire and retain the skills and profiles required for the data journey toward AI and analytics. Is it just treated as one of the many profiles, or is there a special focus reflecting scarceness in the market? If hiring is hard, are there programs for training and upskilling the workforce? How refined are the profile definitions? There should be recognition of the different essential profiles, including data scientist (analytics and machine learning), data engineer (data pre-processing and cleansing), data architect (architectural design of platforms) data 'translators' (translate insights into business relevance) and AI engineers.

BUSINESS ENABLEMENT

The final dimension, which is enabled by all the others, is the business dimension, where the real value creation takes place. Mature organizations have a comprehensive data strategy, where they lay out their plans and objectives for the six dimensions discussed in this chapter. There is also a clear vision of how much needs to be invested in each of the dimensions in order to achieve the goals. A data-mature organization also has a clear view of what use cases are possible and what the expected benefits are (see Chapter 6). Moreover, such organizations measure the economic impact of use cases (see Chapter 7) and report them in a consistent manner at the company level, so that there's a clear understanding of the value generated by the data investments. This is essential for continuing to invest in data.

Finally, apart from applying data and AI internally, to optimize their business, the most data-mature organizations are looking at new business opportunities with data. This could be based on insights generated from company data deemed valuable to other sectors and industries. For example, mobility data generated from mobile antennas — always in an anonymous and aggregated way, and combined with external data — has value for the transport[1], retail[2] and tourism[3] sectors (see Chapter 5). However, the new business opportunity could also be based on partnerships with companies from other sectors to combine data and generate differential insights. Data and AI can also be used for social good — that is, to pursue social objectives such as the UN's SDGs (see Chapter 21).

HOW TO EXECUTE A DATA MATURITY ASSESSMENT

One way to perform a data maturity assessment is to translate each dimension into a set of questions with predefined answers ranging from 1 to 5, where 1 represents little maturity and 5 maximum maturity. This should produce a questionnaire of less than 100 questions, which should be manageable. The questionnaire can be completed through interviews or as a self-assessment, possibly with a session afterward where the self-assessed answers are challenged, and the scores adapted. The resulting scores on each question are then aggregated per dimension, and finally in an overall data-maturity score. If done properly, and avoiding tendencies to 'look good,' this is a powerful tool to manage the data maturity of organizations: it embodies a data-driven way to manage the data journey. It allows the organization to set objectives, track progress over time, prioritize data investments, and compare or benchmark different units, especially in multinational corporations. Still, a fair amount of discipline and process goes into making it happen and keeping it going over the years.

CONCLUSION

In my experience, not many organizations are measuring their data maturity in a systematic way. This is understandable, as it's not a trivial exercise. They trust that they will become more data mature as they progress on their data journey. However, as we'll see in the pages ahead, taking the right data decision often depends on an organization's data maturity, and therefore measuring this explicitly will help to understand and argue why one option should be preferred over others.

THE LONG AND WINDING ROAD
TO DATA MATURITY

**DANIEL
RODRÍGUEZ
SIERRA**
Director of Big Data
& AI, Vodafone

Data maturity is not a state, it is a process. As long as the process is alive, the data maturity journey is ongoing. In a way, it's like happiness: if you stop doing the right things or having the right attitude, it goes away.

I have seen large organizations with a good data culture where most of the objective success factors take regressive steps and lose ground in this journey. I've also seen nimble starters get it right from the onset.

Just like happiness, data maturity is something that's desired by all but hard to define.

I think I can nevertheless say what it is NOT.

Data maturity is not spending millions on the latest technology, to establish a big, fat data platform, or having hundreds of data architects, project managers, data scientists or machine learning engineers building their CVs on outrageously bloated projects that never quite deliver. It is also definitely not *just* about having a data governance council that controls and manages data risk and compliance.

While each is part of it, neither monetary spend nor staff size is the secret to success on its own.

While most experts would give a thumbs-up to things like having plenty of data, other aspects — like team profiles, build-or-buy strategies, and organizational or hierarchical set-up — generate less consensus.

Alternatively, data maturity can be judged by its effects. For instance:
* Core business is about the data, which is the raw material it is built upon.

- Business is not data-native, but runs continuously on data-driven decisions, supported by advanced analytics and machine learning across functions and imbedded into business processes with increasing automation.
- Data unity and affluence: the organization is rich in data and, at its most granular level, there is only one version of it. Functional areas use it in different ways but they have a common, traceable data ancestor.
- Data and insights are mostly self-serviced by company employees.
- Predictions and cause analysis based on behavioural patterns and journeys are leveraged to design and execute customer-facing actions.
- Data is transformed into valuable knowledge following common quality standards that the same organization is able to assess on a regular basis. No black boxes!
- There is a body dedicated to the end-to-end data value chain, from ensuring its acquisition, availability and quality to integrating machine learning results seamlessly into the right processes, with imbedded privacy and security safeguards by design.

5. EXTERNAL MONETIZATION OF DATA

Most organizations with an ambition to become more data-driven start their data journey with internal applications — so-called internal use cases (see Chapter 6). This is where most value can be created in the beginning, and it's also easier to apply new technology to a well-understood business area than to new business. However, this doesn't mean there are no challenges to overcome before the actual value can be realized, as evidenced by many chapters in this book. Once internal use cases are up and running, though, organizations will have gained significant data maturity (see Chapter 4), which makes them ready for the next steps: external monetization.

Until 2020, such new business was only a viable possibility for a few innovative companies. But then, in February 2020, the European Commission published its Data Strategy, launching the concept of European Data Spaces (European Commission, 2020). These are mostly sector-based data spaces repositories that gather data from a varied set of sources (companies, governmental entities) and allow the creation of new products and services, for both business and public administration. We may therefore expect that the notion of 'external monetization' will increase significantly in the coming years.

A NEW VALUE
PROPOSITION

While internal use cases can go beyond increased efficiency, to actually generate more revenues, external monetization enables access to entirely new revenue streams. As part of their normal business operations, many companies create a huge amount of data. Banks generate payment transaction data; telecom operators generate mobility, footfall and social graph data; utility companies generate energy consumption data; supermarkets generate grocery pricing and consumption data; insurance companies generate data about hospitals' performance, car accidents and burglary; and airlines create mobility data. If the company has significant market share, this data can be used to extract valuable insights that can help improve the performance of other businesses or governments.

For example, mobility insights from telecom operators can be used to optimize traffic flow in large cities, or to better understand forced migration patterns. Payment transaction data can be used to build detailed maps of countries' socio-economic status. Energy consumption data can be used to predict when people will be at home for last-mile delivery of ecommerce goods. Hospitals' performance data can be used to optimize the quality and efficiency of a healthcare system.

While still small in overall value, this type of external monetization is a huge strategic opportunity, and organizations are wise to think about this relative to their future strategy. Before companies embark on this endeavour, though, several challenges have to be overcome, and this might be the reason that overall value is relatively minimal.

CHALLENGES

The first challenge is one we have already mentioned: sufficient data maturity. This includes data quality, data governance, data skills, data protection and security, etc. As noted, an organization that's already exploiting data at scale for internal use cases is probably mature enough to start with external monetization.

The second challenge is related to privacy. Much of the data — although not all of it — is generated by customers, and as such is considered personal data. This is protected by various data protection laws, and since May 2018, in Europe, by the GDPR, which gives citizens various new data rights. The need for explicit and informed consent is one of the pillars of the GDPR. In most external monetization scenarios, it is not personal data that is used, but anonymized and aggregated data, which doesn't fall under the GDPR. However, parts of what used to be accepted as anonymized data are considered personal data under the GDPR, which has resulted in stricter anonymous data criteria. Therefore, it is not trivial for organizations to perform the anonymization and aggregation process in such a way that it is legally not considered personal data.

The third challenge is related to reputation. Even when insights are generated from anonymized data and legally everything is fine, many organizations fear a negative impact of everything they do externally with data. Indeed, data scandals abound and are impeding the growth of these opportunities, effectively stunting the many potential positive impacts in businesses, economies and our lives. Using insights generated from anonymized data is quite different from using profiling data for advertising, but the average consumer isn't able to differentiate between the two. Even the news media have difficulty explaining this to the wider society. The Facebook/Cambridge Analytica scandal

— in which consultants to US presidential candidate Donald Trump's 2016 election campaign misused the data of millions of Facebook users — has caused much damage to the sector.

Despite these challenges, companies have decided to create new value from their data assets. In the following section we'll discuss some of the key questions these organizations have faced, and how they resolved them.

HOW TO EXECUTE YOUR EXTERNAL MONETIZATION STRATEGY

A NEW DEPARTMENT?

One of the first decisions that arises is whether the external monetization activity requires creation of a new department, or if it can be run from the existing big data area. It's tempting to think that it should be managed by that already-established centre of expertise. Isn't the raw material the same? The platform investment has already been made. There is already a data governance model in place to assure data quality, the skills are there, and it should be just a matter of hiring more of the same professionals.

While this is all true, there are other factors that point to the need for setting up something new. Table 5.1 gives an analysis of the advantages and disadvantages associated with both options.

	Existing big data department		New business unit	
Concept	*Pros*	*Cons*	*Pros*	*Cons*
Platform	No additional costs	Adapt to external use cases	Built for external use	Additional costs
Skills	Team in place	No businesspeople	E2E profiles	
Budget	Leverage existing investments	Mixing P&L with cost centre	Clean P&L	Some duplication of investments
People	Recognize existing data professionals			Ignoring existing professionals
Innovation		Mixing operation with innovation	Innovate at the edge	Some duplication
SLA		Internal SLA not sufficient for external clients	Client-driven SLA	
Data governance	In place			Define again
Privacy	In place	Only for internal use	Specific for external use of data	
Data sourcing	In place	Focus on internal use cases	Dedicated data sourcing for external use	Some duplication

Table 5.1 Pro and con analysis of leveraging the existing big data department for external monetization versus creating a new dedicated one

There is no one-size-fits-all answer here. But, all in all, it makes sense to start the external monetization effort as part of the existing big data operation. To start the conversation, several basic data capabilities need to be in place before we can even start thinking about what to offer to the market. Much of this work has already been done, for the internal use cases, and can be directly reused. Think about data sourcing, collection, storage, privacy, skills, etc. Moreover, the current big data area will likely be happy to take on such a new, strategic responsibility. A small new team could be hired within the existing area to focus on the specific aspects of external use cases that aren't covered by internal use capabilities. Once ideas and prototypes are in place for testing the market, the existing infrastructure will suffice, as early adopters will start with pilots and non-critical areas. So, the internal SLAs will hold for the moment.

Once the external monetization business is serving its first customers and starting to grow, it might be a good time to spin out the area to a new unit — a department or perhaps even a new company. This requires a profound analysis of what could still be used from the existing area and what needs to be created from the ground up. This may require significant investments, but there is already a business in place to support those investments.

DATA, INSIGHTS OR BUSINESS SOLUTIONS?

Another important question is what exactly will be monetized. Is it the anonymous data as such (duly processed to remove all personally identifiable information)? Are they insights that already have a business value? Or, is it an end-to-end, data-based solution to solve a customer's problem? From data to insights to solutions, we're moving up in the data value chain. **Data** can be used to generate many different insights, but in order to do so, it must be further analysed and combined with business knowledge to come up with these insights. Think of anonymized and aggregated calling data collected from mobile antennas, which can be used for calculating many different things, such as footfall information. **Insights** already have an inherent value and are specific to a certain area. For instance, continuing with the mobile antenna example, we could calculate mobility patterns that provide relevant insights about how crowds of people move around in a certain area, such as a big city. This insight may help to optimize the public transport system. **Business solutions** are one level further up the value chain and solve a specific problem. For instance, if mobility insights are combined with first-party data from a bus or railway organization, this can contribute to a solution for planning a city's public transport system.

In general, the lower in the data value chain, the lower the costs of provisioning ... but also the less value created from a customer perspective. Alternatively, the higher up in the data value chain, the more business value is created, but the provisioning costs are also much higher. This is illustrated in Figure 5.1.

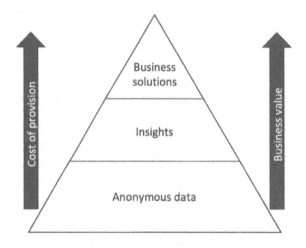

Figure 5.1 Cost and business value for the data value chain

Most organizations are starting to commercialize insights rather than anonymous data or business solutions. This seems to be the sweet spot for a feasible, but still differentiating, solution in the market. Indeed, Telefónica, through its AI & data unit, LUCA, has sold over 400 insights projects in the past few years.

GLOBAL OR LOCAL UNIT?

In multinational corporations, many new business units start at headquarters as a global unit. Once the business starts working, a key question is whether to keep it globally-centralized or to push it out to local business areas that are closer to the markets. Recognizing that there are exceptions, in many multinationals the majority of new business ideas and units start at headquarters. One of the obvious reasons is that it's easier for headquarters than for local businesses to invest in new business ideas. Local businesses are often under tight budget constraints and tremendous pressure for short-term results, which is less the case for headquarters, which is often seen as a cost centre with a mission to strategically invest in the future. With business ideas based on new technologies (such as data and AI), an additional advantage to starting at headquarters is that it's easier to set up a team with scarce skills, since headquarters are usually located in large cities with vibrant hubs of companies, start-ups and universities.

GO TO MARKET

Another key decision when large organizations decide to monetize their data externally is how to approach the market. Basically, there are four main approaches: use existing, local business-to-business (B2B) sales channels; build a dedicated sales force; leverage a mixed central and local sales force; work through a partnership. This is an important decision for any company that decides to set up a new business line, but even more for multinationals with headquarters and local businesses in different geographies. Let's look at each of these options.

Use existing B2B sales channels. Most large organizations have a business-to-consumer (B2C) operation and a separate B2B one, which sells to enterprises and governmental entities. This is usually a well-oiled organization set up to run a professional sales operation with key account managers, a sales pipeline, a proposal preparation area with both technical and business people, and operational teams. The **advantage** of employing this existing sales force is that it's up and running as an organization, has many existing client relationships, and can approach sales of data insights as an upsell, alongside the more traditional offerings. Moreover, adding a new, innovative big data offering to a traditional sales kit gives the B2B unit a modern, innovative air. This is something that the B2B market increasingly values, and sometimes sees as a must.

There are also **disadvantages** associated with the use of existing sales channels. For instance, selling innovative new services like big data requires specific knowledge and skills. Big data and AI are closely related to complex privacy issues, which are not easy to master. Moreover, presenting this type of offering to customers often implies profound conversations rather than just 'sales pitches,' and many traditional B2B sales channels lack the knowledge to go there. Another related disadvantage is that salespeople tend to sell what they best know how to sell, and that doesn't include new, complex offerings. This may lead to lower than expected sales, not because customers aren't interested, but because it is a tougher sales job. The last disadvantage is related to the commissions most sales organizations work with, where sellers are incentivized by getting a percentage of the sale. This gives priority to large-project sales over smaller ones. Since new, innovative big data projects tend to start with small pilots, the corresponding commission is much smaller than what can be earned selling traditional, larger projects.

Setting up a dedicated sales force. In this option, a dedicated sales force is created to sell the new big data offering, as part of a new business unit. Salespeople will be close to, and potentially coming from, the design and development teams of the big data products and services, and therefore knowledgeable about all aspects and challenges (such as privacy matters). As expected, the **advantages** of such an organization are that it mitigates several of the disadvantages that come with using the existing sales force. For example, by design, the lack of knowledge of big data is not an issue here. On the contrary, the specialized salespeople are well informed and enthusiastic about big data products and services. These are the only services they sell, so they're highly motivated to do so. There is therefore no competition with the sales of other, larger projects that would yield higher sales commissions.

As for the **disadvantages**, an existing salesforce has a leg up on a new dedicated sales team, on several levels. First, the new sales organization obviously has to be set up from scratch, which requires time and budget. Additionally, apart from personal networks, it has no existing client relationships, so most meetings will be cold calls, with no opportunity to upsell via existing, trusted relationships. Finally, a dedicated sales team scales much less than an existing sales organization, which might be acceptable in the early phases — when early adopters are approached — but will be a problem when the mainstream market needs to be reached.

Getting the best of both worlds. Having analysed the two previous options, it seems obvious that the best approach for setting up a sales team for big data would be a combined team, leveraging the strengths of both while minimizing their weaknesses. A sales force that has profound knowledge of big data — where part of the team is only incentivized to sell those solutions, and that has many existing, trustworthy relationships with potential customers — seems like a dream team.

In this combined model, there still exists a challenge that needs to be dealt with: alignment of objectives and sales commissions. A combined, local and centralized sales force only works if a win for the local team is also a win for the central team, and the other way around. In other words, regardless of who brings in the initial lead and who closes the deal, the sale is attributed to both teams. Forgetting this 'small' detail will create fierce competition between the two teams, with dramatic (negative) consequences.

By the way, it goes without saying that the worst sales strategy an organization can execute is to have two independent sales forces. In that scenario, you'd have one in the existing local B2B unit and one in the new central unit, competing with each other for customers and commissions, and creating confusion for customers. Still, in the real world nothing is impossible.

Partnering. The last option for setting up a sales force for a big data offering is through partnering with a third-party organization, preferably one that has credibility in the market as an insights provider. In this model, the data holder provides the data in an agreed-upon format, and with a stipulated level of detail (raw, processed or aggregated data) and frequency. It is then the third party that carries the burden of creating the value proposition and doing the actual sales. This option usually implies that the data holder provides raw or processed data, but not insights. That's left to the partner, who's presumed to have a deep understanding of the market. Consequently, the value that the data holder extracts in this model tends to be less per element of data than in the other options, since it is toward the lower end of the data value chain (see Figure 5.1). This is an interesting option for companies that have valuable data but don't have the resources or skills to create the value themselves.

CONCLUSION

There is no one-size-fits-all recommendation on how to approach external monetization. Organizations differ and have diverse cultures. However, in general we can say that, when starting out, it's not a bad idea to begin from the existing big data area. This motivates the existing team and allows for quick pilots and proof of concepts, without requiring large investments. Of course, some changes will have to be made, such as adding people to the team and revisiting privacy matters with legal counsel. This option derives maximum leverage from existing investments.

When business becomes more mature and the client list grows, it makes sense to set up a separate business unit, with its own P&L, and invest more in business development, developing the most effective sales force within the realities of each organization. It is always good to invite some of those who set up the activity to become part of the new business unit, from both a motivational and knowledge perspective.

HOW TO ORGANIZE EXTERNAL MONETIZATION OF DATA

JUAN MURILLO ARIAS
Data Strategy Senior Manager, BBVA Member, European Commission Expert Group on Business to Government (B2G) Data Sharing

Building new business models upon information or data-based insights requires significant lateral thinking to get to the idea that the data you're gathering and curating could be useful beyond the initial purpose for which they were recorded. So, the first stage in this trip is to validate that hypothesis — data usefulness — through early qualitative feedback from those stakeholders who could eventually become end users of your new product.

The second step is to assure that 'privacy by design' principles guide your product design. You will have to answer basic questions, such as, 'Are the data subjects who generated the digital record aware of that use ... and do they agree with it?' Of course, the GDPR legal framework ensures that data are gathered and reused under informed consent and secure flows. However, even with that consent to use personal data, the safest products in this sense are always built upon non-personal data.

The third milestone is to design and develop a product that addresses the questions of as many potential customers as possible. Pilot initiatives can provide enriching learnings to advance in this process, based on quantitative outcomes built upon real data. Keep in mind that it will be quite hard to achieve a one-size-fits-all solution. Key decisions in this sense are the following:

- **How do I structure the information?** When monetizing aggregated insights built upon disaggregated data, the levels of aggregation must be carefully designed in several dimensions, such as geography, time and agents taxonomy. High resolution data aggregations will find their limits in privacy protection thresholds: k-anonymity and l-diversity metrics will have to be fixed.

- **How do I make the information available?** There will be many preferred ways to access data-based insights, depending on end user profiles and technical capabilities: from manual extraction of *.csv formats, to the development of API services that enable automated machine-to-machine interactions, or the integration of insights into interactive dashboards that incorporate graphs and maps.

- **What should be the price of my product?** Just as you can sell flour, baked bread or chocolate muffins at different prices and associated processing costs (that will define your profit margin), raw data, analytical insights or interactive dashboards are very different products, with distinct added value. Setting the price of information on its alternative envelopes can follow two approaches. One is a balance-sheet approach based on the investment made in platforms, development and analysis, its payback period and the expected return on investment. The other is an opportunity-based method: data-based insights will only share a fraction of the value of those decisions that they support, and this will be translated into the price that the end user will be able to pay.

Last, but not least, some mistakes to be avoided:

- **Do not overestimate the value of your data.** That value does not lie in how new your data source is or how fancy the big data or AI brands, but on the real utility they provide against the incumbent methods you're trying to replace (for example, surveys). Leverage the volume, representativity, quick availability and affordability strengths, and be quite transparent on these characteristics to create trust in your product.

- **Do not underestimate barriers on this path.** You will find that development and quality assurance testing take longer than expected. Make a trade-off between: a) the need to release an MVP (minimum viability data product) to enable kick-testing; b) the amount of technical debt that's acceptable not to erode the reliability of your product at its early stage. Besides, you'll discover that many end users are comfortable in their BAU ways of working and will not surrender and pivot toward other targets with more innovative mindsets.

Thinking outside the box is always associated with uncertainty and risk-taking, but when innovation becomes successful, game-changing results are achieved.

INTERNAL VERSUS EXTERNAL DATA MONETIZATION: HOW TO EXTRACT VALUE FROM DATA

**ELENA GIL
LIZASOAIN**
Director, Product &
Business Operations,
Telefónica IoT &
Big Data

Companies across all industries, from startups to large enterprises, are exploring the transformative power of combining big data and AI. Those that don't capitalize on it — to derive meaningful insights and convert them into action — will lose competitiveness and risk being left behind in the new data-driven landscape.

However, the implementation of AI in business can be approached in many ways, and there are a few data monetization strategies to choose from. One of the first dilemmas companies face is deciding whether to monetize data internally or externally (or both). How do they choose the right approach and where should they concentrate their efforts?

The internal path focuses on leveraging data to have a measurable impact on the revenues and bottom line of the company. Some internal monetization initiatives include identifying cross- and up-selling opportunities, personalizing products and services, churn prediction or improving company operations and productivity. On the other hand, external monetization involves creating new revenue streams by making data/insights available to customers and partners through different data-sharing and business models.

Here are some takeaways learned while helping leading organizations adopt their strategies, including Telefónica's own experience:

First, the top priority should be clear alignment of AI projects with the big-picture strategic goals of the company. Successful data monetization requires a careful approach, geared toward achieving the highest-value opportunities that are consistent with the company's overall business strategy.

Next, for most businesses, the implementation of a successful AI strategy starts internally, since the business case is normally higher and has direct impact in the short term. Even though internal and external monetization aren't mutually exclusive, and some companies accomplish both, internal efforts are typically a solid path to external monetization.

Nevertheless, those companies deciding to pursue external data monetization need to address additional challenges and pitfalls as a counterbalance to the potential monetary value. The top priority should be guaranteeing customers and other stakeholders that data privacy and security are accounted for, preventing corporate reputation damage.

This was the approach successfully followed by Telefónica in its AI journey. The strategy was to combine the primary focus on internal projects with the launch of LUCA, Telefónica's external data division, which is tasked with helping private and public organizations in their digital transformation by supplying business insights that leverage anonymized and aggregated telco data.

PART II

BUSINESS AND FINANCE

The second part of this book is about business and finance. We will look at some key decisions associated with selecting use cases, measuring economic value, and how corporations should think about financing the investments in data and AI. Finally, we'll discuss the role of open data, and how AI and big data can add value to small- and medium-sized enterprises (SMEs).

This part is not about explaining to business people what big data and AI are. Nor is it about specific examples of big data and AI use cases. Numerous other books explain what these technologies entail and how they can serve to improve and optimize businesses. Instead, as already mentioned, this part is about important data-related decisions that affect business or finance.

6. HOW TO SELECT AI AND BIG DATA USE CASES

Many organizations that set out to work with big data and AI ask themselves where they should start. In general, there are two ways: start building the necessary capabilities (infrastructure, data, skills, etc.); start with use cases that show the potential value to the organization, and see what data is needed for execution. Most organizations choose the second approach, since it's easier to invest in capabilities once there is a clearer understanding of the value that can be generated.

But how can you choose the best use cases to start with? In our experience, the best way to attack this problem is by building an opportunity matrix, also called the Ansoff Matrix (Wikipedia, n.d.), with the specific data and AI opportunities for the organization.

OPPORTUNITY MATRIX

Let's say you want to use Robotic Process Automation (RPA) as part of your digital strategy, and you need to determine what process to start with. The most successful applications of RPA are on processes that are highly structured and relate to the core business. Figure 6.1 illustrates what such a matrix could look like, where the size of the circle represents the business value, and the greyscale colour the risk involved (light grey for little risk, medium for moderate risk, dark for high risk). The horizontal axis represents the business centricity and the vertical axis how structured the process is. The ideal process to start with would be the large, light grey one in the top right.

AUTOMATION OPPORTUNITY MATRIX

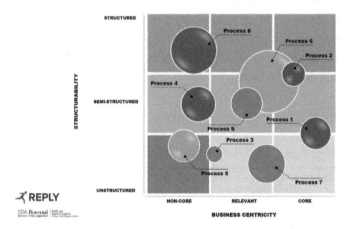

Figure 6.1 Generic Opportunity Matrix for RPA applications (SDA Bocconi, 2019)

But how do we apply the opportunity matrix to data and AI use cases for organizations that want to start? The two main axes usually represent **value** or **business impact** and **feasibility**. Value is important because demonstrating a use case on something that's of lateral importance to the business doesn't convince the organization to invest. Feasibility is important because the results should not come in two years, but in months — the patience of businesses for new things to show results is limited. However, other dimensions can be used for the axes (such as **urgency** to act);

this depends on what's most important for the organization at the time of starting. The additional dimensions (size, form, and colour) should represent other important factors to consider in the decision process.

Figure 6.2 illustrates an opportunity matrix for big data use cases for the digital services of Telefónica Digital in 2012. We prioritized the digital services that should have big data (business intelligence) capabilities according to value and urgency. The size of the bubble represents how simple it was to work on the service (less complexity), resulting in quicker results. The greyscale represents the risk of creating a silo solution as opposed to the preferable integrated solution, where data of all digital services was stored in a single big data platform.

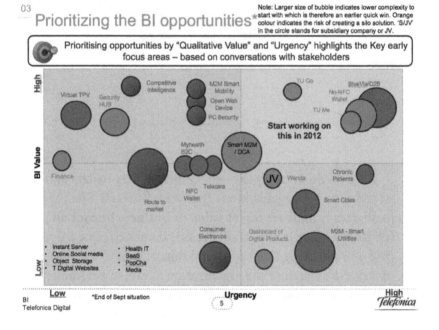

Figure 6.2 Big data use cases opportunity matrix for Telefónica Digital in 2012

Sometimes it is hard to **estimate the business value** of a use case before actually executing it. A good way to estimate that value is to multiply the business volume with the estimated percentage of optimization (see Chapter 7). For instance, if the churn rate of a company is 1% per month, and there are about 10 million customers, with a monthly average revenue per user (ARPU) of €10, the business volume amounts to €1million per month, or €12million a year. If big data could reduce the churn rate by 25% — that is, from 1% to 0.75% — the estimated value would be €250,000 a month.

The other important dimension to estimate is the **feasibility** of use cases. This is a more qualitative estimation, which might be different across various organizations. Basically, it estimates how easy or difficult it is to execute the use case, including factors such as availability of data (location, ownership, cost), quality of data, degree of collaboration with the business area (some are champions, others are defensive; see Chapter 16), privacy risk, etc.

FINDING USE CASES

So, how can you get an overview of **what use cases** to consider for your industry? Many organizations have an initial idea of some use cases, such as upselling or churn reduction, but might lack the deeper understanding necessary to come up with a more exhaustive list to consider. Luckily, there is enough sector-based literature to help organizations with this step. For the telecom industry, for example, the TM Forum maintains a list of about a hundred use cases (TM Forum, 2015) along with important characteristics, such as data requirements, privacy risk, value, etc. For the insurance industry, Figure 6.3 provides an overview of many AI use cases.

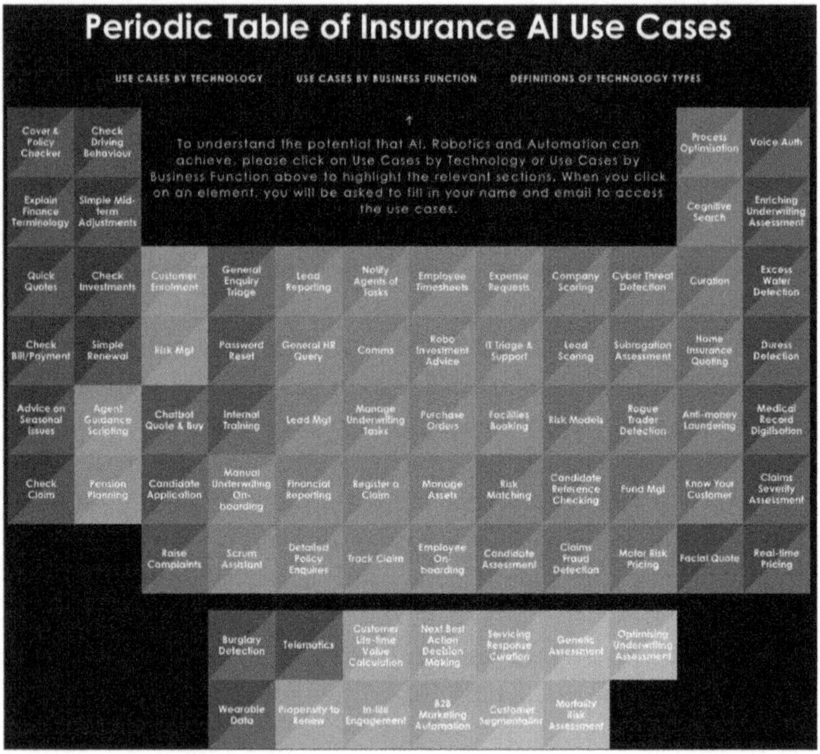

Periodic Table of Insurance AI Use Cases

USE CASES BY TECHNOLOGY   USE CASES BY BUSINESS FUNCTION   DEFINITIONS OF TECHNOLOGY TYPES

To understand the potential that AI, Robotics and Automation can achieve, please click on Use Cases by Technology or Use Cases by Business Function above to highlight the relevant sections. When you click on an element, you will be asked to fill in your name and email to access the use cases.

Cover & Policy Checker · Check Driving Behaviour · Process Optimisation · Voice Auth

Explain Finance Terminology · Simple Mid-term Adjustments · Cognitive Search · Enriching Underwriting Assessment

Quick Quotes · Check Investments · Customer Enrolment · General Enquiry Triage · Lead Reporting · Notify Agents of Tasks · Employee Timesheets · Expense Requests · Company Scoring · Cyber Threat Detection · Curation · Excess Water Detection

Check Bill/Payment · Simple Renewal · Risk Mgt · Password Reset · General HR Query · Comms · Robo Investment Advice · IT Triage & Support · Lead Scoring · Subrogation Assessment · Home Insurance Quoting · Duress Detection

Advice on Seasonal Issues · Agent Guidance Scripting · Chatbot Quote & Buy · Internal Training · Lead Mgt · Manage Underwriting Tasks · Purchase Orders · Facilities Booking · Risk Models · Rogue Trader Detection · Anti-money Laundering · Medical Record Digitisation

Check Claim · Pension Planning · Candidate Application · Manual Underwriting On-boarding · Financial Reporting · Register a Claim · Manage Assets · Risk Matching · Candidate Reference Checking · Fund Mgt · Know Your Customer · Claims Severity Assessment

Raise Complaints · Scrum Assistant · Detailed Policy Enquiries · Track Claim · Employee On-boarding · Candidate Assessment · Claims Fraud Detection · Motor Risk Pricing · Facial Quote · Real-time Pricing

Burglary Detection · Telematics · Customer Life-time Value Calculation · Next Best Action Decision Making · Servicing Response Curation · Genetic Assessment · Optimising Underwriting Assessment

Wearable Data · Propensity to Renew · In-life Engagement · B2B Marketing Automation · Customer Segmentation · Mortality Risk Assessment

Figure 6.3 AI use cases for the insurance industry

Source http://wisetothenew.com/ai/

Then there are also the usual research reports, detailing many use cases for different sectors, such as the McKinsey report on AI (Bughin et al., 2017) focusing on Retail, Utilities, Manufacturing, Healthcare and Education, and the PwC report, 'Sizing the Price' (Rao and Verweij, 2019). If you're looking for AI use cases in a particular sector, you can, of course, simply search online, which will provide many suggestions, as illustrated in Figure 6.4.

Q   artificial intelligence use cases|

Q   artificial intelligence use case - Google Search

Q   artificial intelligence use cases

Q   artificial intelligence use cases pdf

Q   artificial intelligence use cases in banking

Q   artificial intelligence use cases in manufacturing

Q   artificial intelligence use cases in insurance

Q   artificial intelligence use cases in agriculture

Q   artificial intelligence use cases in retail

Q   artificial intelligence use cases in telecom

Q   artificial intelligence use cases in healthcare

Figure 6.4 Finding the AI use cases in your sector

HOW TO NOT FAIL WITH USE CASES

ANTONIO PITA LOZANO
Global Head of AI & Analytics, Telefónica IoT & Big Data Tech

The selection of use cases forms an important part of companies' transformation to become data-driven, but these often don't achieve the expected result, causing disappointment and slowing down the transformation process.

In some cases, we come across failed use cases that 'blow up' the company's entire transformation effort. For this reason, I always recommend performing an analysis after the implementation of each use case, which helps identify lessons learned for improving the results of the next use cases.

After analysing many use cases implemented in various companies, I identified a main cause of failure. It basically comes down to mismanagement of expectations. And, if we delve a little deeper into the underlying reasons, we can see that most failures stem from inadequate alignment of the use case's requirements with the data maturity of the organization. This is seen in the three pillars of a data-driven organization: technology, talent, and organization and culture.

Analytical use cases are a challenge by themselves, so we must avoid working in parallel on the use case and advancing the data-driven pillars.

- Regarding the technological pillar, it is important to confirm that the technologies required by the use case are actually available in the company. If the use case requires a new technology, it helps to carry out the process in two steps. First, make the required technology available in the company with another simple, well known and easy to implement use case. Only then, once there's some experience with the new technology, should you implement the analytical use case of interest. It is important to note that implementing a complex analytical use case with a technology that's new to the organization significantly increases the risk of failure.

- Regarding the talent pillar, it is important to have a map of all internal capabilities, and to ensure that all skills required for the use case are present in the company. If not, the missing capabilities should be put in place (either internally or through external partnering) and tested on another simple, easy-to-evaluate use case that will generate professional trust among all team members. If a problem is detected in a new use case that's being implemented by a new team, the seeds of distrust will be sown.

- Concerning the organization and culture pillar, it's important to ensure that the company is 'data mature' enough to properly value the knowledge extracted from the data and act on it, having the appropriate processes and the required culture. In my experience, change generates rejection, especially when it is related to complex scientific issues. Furthermore, because predicting the future is impossible, predictive models will fail in some cases, leading to fear of failure that can paralyse the evolution of the use case.

In summary, the maturity of a company's data-driven pillars will determine which use cases are likely to succeed or fail. If the organization is in an early stage of the data-driven journey, it is advisable to select simple use cases that require little technological implementation and affect the least number of functional processes. In addition, it makes sense to select use cases that have been successful in other companies in the sector. Conversely, if the maturity of an organization's data-driven pillars is high, it is possible to opt for more innovative use cases and take the risk. The company will in fact embrace and reward that risk.

Sometimes, companies have heterogeneous levels of maturity in the different data pillars. For example, they could be strong in technology and talent, but weak in cultural transformation. In such instances, it is essential to identify the strengths and select those use cases that leverage them, while rejecting those that depend on the less advanced data pillars.

If you want to be successful with the development of analytical use cases in your company, remember to align them with the state of maturity of the pillars of a data-driven company.

7. HOW TO MEASURE ECONOMIC IMPACT

How do we put an economic value on big data initiatives in our organizations? How can we measure the impact of such projects in our businesses? How can we convince senior leadership to continue (and increase) their investment in this area?

Most of us who are familiar with the big data boom are also familiar with the big, bold promises made about its value for our economies and society. For example, McKinsey estimated in 2011 that big data would bring $300 billion in value for healthcare, €250 billion for the European public sector and $800 billion for global personal location data (Manyika et al., 2011). McKinsey subsequently published an estimate of what percentage of that anticipated value had become a reality as of December 2016 (Henke et al., 2016). It suggested that the actual value was up 30%, and up 50-60% for location-based data.

These astronomic numbers are convincing many organizations to start their big data journey. Back in 2017, *Forbes* (Press, 2017) estimated that the market value for big data and analytics technology would grow from $130 billion in 2016 to $203 billion in 2020. As with many of these predictions, one has to wonder who's checking whether they have come true.

Indeed, these sky-high numbers do not tell individual companies and institutions how to measure the value they generate with their big data initiatives. Many organizations are struggling to assign an economic value to their big data investments, which is one of the main reasons so many initiatives aren't reaching their ambitious goals.

So, how can we put numbers on big data and analytics initiatives? From my experience, there are three main sources of economic value. Let's take a look at these.

REDUCING COSTS WITH BIG DATA IT INFRASTRUCTURE

There are considerable savings to be made on IT infrastructure, from propriety software to open source. The traditional data warehouse model of IT providers of data is to charge a license fee for the software part, and charge separately for the needed professional services. In addition, some solutions come with specific hardware, as so-called appliances.

Before the age of big data, this model worked well. However, with the increasing amount of data, much of which is non-structured and real time, existing solutions have become prohibitively expensive. This, combined with a so-called 'vendor lock-in' — as investments and complexity make it costly and difficult to change to another vendor solution — has forced many organizations to look for more economical solutions.

One of the original, popular alternatives is provided by the open source Hadoop (Hadoop, 2020) ecosystem of big data management tools. Open source software has no license cost and is therefore quite attractive. However, to be able to take advantage of open source solutions for big data, organizations need to have the appropriate skills and experience, either in-house or outsourced.

The Hadoop ecosystem tools run on commodity software, scale linearly and are therefore much more cost effective.

For these reasons, many organizations have substituted part of their propriety data infrastructure with open source, potentially saving up to millions of euros annually. While saving on IT doesn't give you the greatest economic value, it is relatively easy to measure in the Total Cost of Ownership (TCO) of your data infrastructure, so it's a popular strategy to start with.

ANALYTICS USE CASES
TO OPTIMIZE YOUR BUSINESS

There is no question that big data and analytics can improve your core business. There are two ways to achieve such economic benefits: by generating additional revenues or reducing costs.

Generating additional revenues means doing more with the same — in other words, using big data to drive revenue. The problem here is that it isn't easy to decide where to start, and it can be hard to work out how to measure the 'doing more.'

Reducing costs means doing the same with less — using big data to make business processes more efficient, while maintaining the same results.

As discussed in Chapter 6, a good strategy involves starting your big data journey with a use case opportunity-feasibility matrix, which plots the value (business impact) against how feasible it is to realize that value. We also saw in Chapter 6 that a good way to estimate the business value of a use case is to multiply business volume by estimated percentage of optimization. As we saw, for a *revenue generation use case* like churn prediction, if the churn rate of a company is 1% (per month) and there are about 10 million customers, with average monthly revenue per user of €10, then the business volume amounts to €1 million per month, or €12 million a year. If big data could reduce the churn rate by 25% (from 1% to 0.75%), the estimated value would be €250,000 per month. As an example of a *cost saving use case*, consider procurement. Suppose an organization spends €100 million on procurement every year. Analytics might lead to a 0.5% optimization, which would amount to a potential value of €500,000 a year.

However, once the initial use cases have been selected, how should you measure the benefits? This is all about comparing the situation before and after, measuring the difference, and knowing how to extrapolate its value if it were applied as BAU. Over the years, we've learned that there are two main issues that make it hard to measure and disseminate the economic impact of big data in an organization:

1. Big data and AI are almost never the only contributors to an improvement. Other business areas will be involved, making it difficult to decide how much value to assign to big data and AI.

2. There may be reluctance to tell top management, and the whole organization, about the results obtained. Giving exposure to the value of big data is fundamental in raising awareness and creating a data-driven culture in your company.

With regard to point 1, big data is almost never the sole driver of value creation. Let's again consider the churn use case, and assume you use analytics to better identify which customers are most likely to leave in the next month. Once these customers have been identified, other parts of the company need to define a retention campaign, and yet another department executes the campaign. For example, they might physically call the top 3,000 people at risk and pitch an attractive 'stay with us' offer. Once the campaign is done, and the results are there, it's hard to decide whether the results, or what part of them, are due to analytics, due to the retention offer or due the execution by the call centres.

There are two ways to deal with this issue:

1. Start with use cases that have never been done before. An example would be to use real-time, contextual campaigns. Such campaigns aren't frequently used in many industries, as they require expensive big data technology. Imagine you're a mobile customer with a data tariff, watching a video. The use case is to detect in real time that you are watching a video and that you have almost reached the limit of your data bundle. In these instances, you're typically either throttled or disconnected from the internet. Either situation results in a bad customer experience. In the new situation enabled by the use case, you would receive a message in real time telling you about your bundle ending, and asking you whether you want to buy an extra 500MB, for perhaps €2. If you accepted this offer, the service would be provisioned in real time, and you would be able to continue watching your video. The value of this use case is easy to calculate: simply take the number of customers that have accepted the offer, and multiply it by the price charged to the customer. Since there is no previous experience with this use case, few people will challenge you that the value is not due to big data and analytics.

2. Compare that with what would happen if you didn't use analytics. The second solution is a bit more complex, but applies more often than the previous case. Let's go back to the churn example. It's unlikely that an organization has *never* done anything about retention, either in a basic or more sophisticated way. So, when you undertake your analytics initiative to identify customers who are likely to leave the company, and you have a good result,

you can't just say that it's all due to analytics. You need to compare it with what would have happened without analytics, all other things being equal. This requires using control groups. When you select a target customer set for your campaign, you should reserve a small, random part of this group to treat exactly the same as the target customers, but without the analytics part. Then, any statistically significant difference between the target set and the control group can be ascribed to the influence of analytics. For instance, if with analytics you retain 2% more customers than the control group, you then calculate how much revenue you would retain annually, if the retention campaign would be run every month. Some companies are able to run control groups for every single campaign, and are always able to calculate the 'uplift,' and continuously report the economic value that can be assigned to analytics. However, most companies will only do control groups in the beginning, to confirm the business case. Once confirmed, they consider it BAU, and a new baseline has been created.

With regard to point 2, sharing results attributable to big data within the organization — in the right way — is fundamental. It's been our experience that while business owners love analytics for the additional revenues or cost reduction, they might initially be reluctant to tell the rest of the organization about it. In fact, evangelizing about the success of internal big data projects is key to getting top management on board and changing the culture.

Why would individual business owners hesitate in sharing? The reason is simple: they're human. Showing the wider organization that using big data and analytics creates additional revenue makes some business owners worry about getting higher targets, but not with more resources (apart from big data). Similarly, business owners might not

want to share a cost saving of 5%, since it might reduce their
next budget accordingly. After all, haven't they shown that
with big data they can achieve the same goals with less?
This is an example of a cultural challenge. Luckily, these
things tend not to happen in stealth mode for long, and in
the end, all organizations get used to publishing the value.
But, any time spent doing this 'underground' might be a
problem, especially at the beginning of the big data journey,
when such economic results are most needed.

TAPPING NEW REVENUE
STREAMS THROUGH EXTERNAL
DATA MONETIZATION

In Chapter 5, we introduced external data monetization
as a way to tap into new sources of revenue, instead of
generating value through business optimization. As we
explained, this opportunity is appropriate for organizations
that have reached a certain level of data maturity (see Chapter 4). Once they're ready to exploit the benefits of big data
to optimize their business, they can start looking to create
new business around data. This can be achieved either by
creating new data value propositions (i.e. new products
with data at their heart), or by creating insights from big
data to help other organizations optimize their business. In
this sense, measuring the economic value of data, analytics
and AI is not all that different than launching new products
in the market and managing their P&L.

We believe that in the coming five years, the lion's share
of the value of big data will still come from business optimization — that is, by turning companies and institutions into
data-driven organizations that take data-driven decisions.
But with a growing interest in and activity of data sharing,

as shown by the European Data Strategy,[1] launched in February 2020, business opportunities through external monetization are set to grow significantly.

CONCLUSION

As we've seen, in order to measure the economic impact of data and AI, savings from IT are a good starting point, but will not scale with the business. Revenues from external data monetization and data sharing are also easy to measure, but are still modest compared to the value that can be generated from internal use cases for business optimization.

For those who don't ultimately succeed in measuring any concrete economic impact, don't worry. Experience teaches us that while organizations in the early phase of their journey are obsessed with measuring value, more mature organizations know that the value is there and don't feel the need to continue micro-measuring improvements. At this point, big data will have become fully integrated and be seen as BAU.

HOW TO MEASURE ECONOMIC IMPACT IN A DATA-DRIVEN COMPANY

MARKUS HEIMANN
Telefónica Germany GmbH & Co. OHG
Director Digital & Data Competence Centre (DDC), incl. Wayra Germany

Becoming a data-driven company requires many changes, on many different levels. Besides the technical requirements that must be established, we need to change the corporate culture and the skills of the employees. One of our biggest challenges was implementing the idea of data democratization, which means offering all data and information (excluding sensitive, legally regulated stock market-related information) to our 8,000 employees in Germany.

The objective was to break down barriers to providing the data to every employee for his or her daily work, to optimize client-related decisions and internal processes in real time. It was important that we offer our data and information in a self-service portal, which could be used easily. Accordingly, in 2016 we launched the Analytical Insights Centre (AIC), which is today used by more than 2,500 Telefónica employees in Germany.

The plan to democratize data only works if the data is accepted, understood and has sufficient quality for data scientists to effectively utilize it. We developed this self-service environment for different analytic skills, ranging from junior data analyst to hardcore data scientist. After introducing the big data infrastructure, tech experts, the data labs and data governance professionals asked us: how can we measure the economic impact of our data strategy?

The value-based project approach was particularly efficient. For every analytical project, we defined a specific use case with clear scope and a measurable target. For example: reduction of the churn rate of x% based on improving the machine-learning algorithm to identify early on who wants to withdraw their contract. And, in parallel: improving the calculation of the next-best activity or offer for these critical customers. To be successful, we found that it's absolutely necessary that the project team consist of a competence centre and specialists from the different business units. The whole team must have the same financial target, and stay together as a team until that target is reached.

Another good example is our activity to optimize the handling of technical network incidents, which inevitably occur in a complex mobile telecom network of more than 27,000 sites across Germany. We employ AI algorithms in a variety of use cases — for example, to predict recurring incidents or the expected duration of incident resolution. Thus, we can reduce the number of field force assignments while speeding up the resolution of incidents. The downtime of network elements is reduced, which leads to increased customer satisfaction. Based on these KPIs, it's easy to measure the economic impact.

In terms of revenue assurance, we used our machine-learning environment to extract large amounts of data — like hundreds of thousands of change tickets for the operational systems, millions of customer profiles, billions of call detail records — spanning multiple complex IT systems to identify issues that may cause significant revenue losses, which can be measured in Euros. Having identified these issues in turn allows us to address them and avoid lost revenue.

Our Marketing Performance Management Model is another good example to show how you can measure the impact of data-driven solutions. This is a sophisticated driver model, which identifies and quantifies the impact of specific marketing levers on our business performance in winning new customers for our brands, such as O2. With multiple marketing levers at the disposal of Telefónica Germany (e.g. media spends), it is important to ensure that the available budget is allocated to these levers in an optimal way.

This is especially true when the number of customers is measured in millions, as they are in the telecom business.

Employing these results allows us to optimize the marketing spend and lever mix, which contributes to winning additional new customers and increasing revenue. The impact could be shown by the business improvement after introducing the model.

8. HOW TO FUND YOUR DATA JOURNEY

As of 2020, most large multinationals had started their journey to become a more data-driven organization, usually as part of their digital transformation. For most of them, it was clear that starting a data journey requires funding: a team had to be created and a data infrastructure (cloud or on-premise) needed to be available. The first pilot projects would be selected, usually together with several of the business areas. If the pilot was successful, it would be put into production to obtain the data benefits on a structural basis. For instance, for a churn pilot, the data team gets a customer data set from Marketing and predicts with machine-learning techniques which customers are at risk of defecting to the competition. Marketing then tries to retain them. The number of retained customers can be translated into retained revenues (see Chapter 7). Putting this into production requires that the customer data set is provided every week or month, the algorithms are executed automatically, and the result is fed into the appropriate channels to facilitate customer outreach.

At the beginning of the journey, there isn't usually much discussion of who pays for what. What's important is that things are happening and moving forward. But, when the team grows — and more pilots see the light of day and need to be put into production — questions about funding arise.

Should the corporation continue to invest in the team? Should the relevant line of business pay for all or part of it? If corporate keeps funding it, should the business be charged? If so, at what rate? If the work involves a third-party company, who is paying for its services? Moreover, multinationals are usually formed by different legal entities, and doing things for 'free' is not easy to handle from a tax and anti-competition perspective.

ALTERNATIVE MODELS
TO FUND DATA INVESTMENTS

There are no unique answers to these questions, but we can see some patterns related to the data maturity of the organizations. In general, as illustrated in Figure 8.1, corporate funding is available in the beginning, and over time, with increasing data maturity, central funding goes down and business unit funding goes up. Usually, a small part of central funding remains to explore and test innovative new technology and use cases.

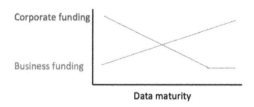

Figure 8.1 Typical funding evolution of data initiatives

A specific application of this funding strategy is that the corporation pays for the central initiative for a few years so the businesses get used to it, and from a certain decision point, joint funding commences, as illustrated in Figure 8.2. The advantage of this joint funding model is that corporate can still stimulate strategically relevant local investments, but business units need to invest also, avoiding the pitfall that 'gifts' are easily accepted but not put into practice.

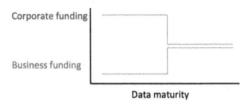

Figure 8.2 Funding starts central and, at some point in time, it becomes joint funding

Looking at the different stages of a data initiative — pilot, deployment and production — there are two main models where corporate funding diminishes over time, as illustrated in Figure 8.3 and Figure 8.4.

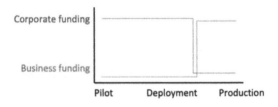

Figure 8.3 Corporation funds pilot and deployment, business funds production

In earlier stages of the data journey, the corporation might fund the data initiative in its pilot and deployment stages, and the business unit takes care of funding the production part (Figure 8.3).

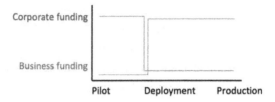

Figure 8.4 Corporation funds pilot, business funds deployment and production

However, it is more common that the corporation only funds the pilot part, which will be reusable among many lines of business. Deployment and production elements are then fully funded by the units, as they are business-specific and not reusable (Figure 8.4). The latter strategy is also more acceptable from a tax perspective, keeping only the group functions at the corporate level.

As a creative funding approach, the corporation can use the availability of free data assets to stimulate the business to step up its efforts in the data journey. For instance, this can come in the form of investing in data quality or governance, or adopting a centrally developed data model. This implies that corporate continues to fund data initiatives, but businesses can only take advantage if they comply with the top-down data strategy and standards. This model is illustrated in Figure 8.5.

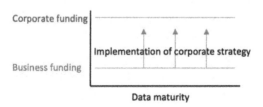

Figure 8.5 Stimulating local businesses to comply with a corporate data strategy

There are, however, also situations where the first funding comes from the business, and the corporation steps in at a later stage. This is the case when a leading business in the group explores a data initiative on its own, and the result is considered a best practice. In this case, the business has funded the pilot and the deployment, and the corporation then helps turn the successful initiative into an asset that can be reused by the other lines of businesses. This situation is illustrated in Figure 8.6.

Figure 8.6 Funding starts by a leading business unit;
the corporation then steps in to fund development of a reusable asset
that can be deployed by other businesses in the group

HOW MUCH TO INVEST IN DATA AND AI?

In my experience, one of the key lessons learned for funding the data and AI journey is to make visible at a local and global level how much budget is invested in data. From that moment data stops being something intangible, with lofty promises, and is recognized as something that can be managed explicitly. Is the company globally investing too much or too little in data? Are the investments by the local units proportional to the size of the local business, or are some over-investing and others short-changing the effort?

Suddenly, all these questions become answerable. I would assert that this is one of the most relevant decision points in the data journey, where there is a before and an after.

One way for organizations to make this happen is to require local businesses to include a compulsory section on data in their annual strategic planning process. How much does the business plan want to invest in data-related initiatives and technology? How much return is expected? What are the main use cases that require the budget and generate the return on investment? Once an organization is able to answer these questions as part of its normal processes, it has taken a major step forward in becoming data-driven.

Making all data-related investments visible is no trivial matter. Many such investments are often 'hidden' in IT projects or external contracts with vendors, and were originally not categorized as data-related, so a lot of analysis and effort are necessary to make this explicit. Moreover, an initiative, technology or project often isn't data- or IT-specific, but is both. The IT system generates data, so from a functional perspective it is an IT project, but from a data perspective it is a data project. How, then, do we assign the appropriate percentage to data and IT?

Every organization is different, and there's no right or wrong amount to invest in data, or formula for what the percentage of data versus IT should be. In my experience, for a large multinational corporation operating in more than 20 geographical locations, investments are in the order of many tens of millions of dollars or euros. In terms of the proportion of data versus IT, the range I have seen is 5-10%.

CONCLUSION

My personal observation has been that large organizations have a limited amount of patience as they await tangible financial results of their data and AI investments (and not only for data and AI initiatives). If patience runs out before there are sufficient results, the data and AI area runs the risk of a major reorganization or significant downscaling. The typical time frame before organizations start to question the investment is 18-24 months. A piece of advice for the Chief Data Officer, the Chief AI Officer or the Chief Analytics Officer is therefore to focus efforts on having visible financial results within this time frame. After 18 months without such results, expect a less-than-pleasant call from senior management.

The following six months (i.e. between 18 and 24 months) are then of critical importance to be able to show those results. If that happens, the organization will likely be happy to continue investment ... provided there is a clear plan. If no convincing results are available, an overhaul of the data and AI initiative is probably in the making.

Finally, here's a small, practical lesson learned in case everything fails. Try to keep track of all analytics and AI initiatives across the organization, in terms of how far they have come in generating actual value. We used to use a spreadsheet to track all initiatives that came out of the process for selecting use cases (Chapter 6), with the following fields:

- Name of the initiative and brief description
- Business owner
- Commitment of the business owner to perform a pilot
- Result of the pilot in terms of financial impact
- Estimated business impact if pilot would be put into production
- Plan of the business owner to put pilot into production

- Pilot actually put into production
- Reporting of annual financial impact of system in production

This will give organizations a bottom-up view of what has
been done, and what financial return has been measured,
recognizing that it's impossible to measure all initiatives (as
discussed in Chapter 7). If organizations maintain such a
list with discipline, something can be presented whenever
management asks for financial results of data, analytics or
Al initiatives. As we all know, it is so much easier to ask for
a budget when you can show tangible results immediately.

DATA-DRIVEN MARKETING AND SALES IN THE B2B MARKET

DANIEL GOBERNA
Director, Commercial Planning & Business Intelligence, Telefónica Cyber & Cloud Tech

A modern approach to B2B marketing requires a data-driven approach across the entire customer and prospect lifecycle.

Start with market identification: for each operating business, it is necessary to identify 100% of the B2B market, including both customers and prospects, and assess their potential value, their expected expenditure, how digitized they are, etc. This allows them to set commercial targets according to the real size of the pie and not based on sales reps' intuition, ambition or simply historical sales.

To improve customer acquisition effectiveness, prospects should be prioritized according to their propensity to buy, and leveraging buyer intent data, the sales team can convey the right value proposition at the right moment.

For existing customers, focus on wallet share. This reveals opportunities for upselling and cross-selling, avoiding shortsightedness in segmentation, where a customer seen as small and therefore underserved is indeed much larger, because he's buying the bulk of his needs from a competitor. 'Next Best Action' models drive customer interactions: to upsell if customers show the right profile and propensity; or to retain at-risk customers according to churn models and recent touchpoint interactions.

To start the journey to become a data-driven organization, there are three main challenges to address. Let's take a look at them.

1. Build a data lake that combines internal and external sources to depict a 360 view of the market, including both customers and prospects:

a) This is the hardest part; it can be frustrating, with a lot of effort at the beginning and no return in the short term. But, it is a key enabler and an essential condition. Extract all the value from your own data, transactional data, and especially data from your customer touchpoints, both structured and unstructured.

b) Sometimes we get more and better information from external sources than from internal ones, even for our own customers! Leverage open data. There are a lot of potential free, public and data sets ready for you to use, which will deliver value for your business.

2. Data gets its real value depending on how you use it. The same data set could be useless or incredibly valuable. It's all about creativity in building relevant use cases. Creativity arises through the confluence of different profiles, with different skills and backgrounds. Data scientists and data engineers should be aware of business challenges in order to suggest potential uses of the models they build. More importantly, business experts should be aware of data science possibilities, or they won't be able to envision a given business challenge being effectively addressed through AI technology. In this regard, there's considerable value in data science tools for non-experts that allow business users to quickly prototype their own AI and ML models without writing a single line of code.

3. Finally, we should make the results of AI and machine-learning models available to the right people, through the right channels and at the right time. The best model and data set won't generate any impact if they aren't used at the moments of truth with customers and prospects. Invest in integration with CRM systems to ensure that leads flow seamlessly from the analytical engine to the hands of the sales rep who has to monetize it.

Communication and engagement with the sales team is key. Set the right expectations to avoid premature disappointment and support them to make sure that they're able to extract all possible value from the analytical model.

9. HOW TO APPROACH OPEN DATA

Companies that have started their data journey will sooner or later come across the notion of open data. Some will just pass, while others will start to explore what it is and how it could be useful on their data journey. While there's limited company experience with open data, this chapter provides some observations and learnings from the experience of a few large companies.

While many aspects of the journey to become data-driven are similar for enterprises and governmental agencies, and we therefore use the term 'organization' in this book, for open data the journey is very different. This is simply because public administrations in many countries are required to publish their data as open data, while for companies this obligation doesn't exist. However, the journey is similar for *using* open data to improve one's functioning.

Open data is a particular part of data sharing. In general, there are four types of data sharing in this context:
- Government-to-Business data sharing (G2B) happens when companies use open data from governments.
- Government-to-Government data sharing (G2G) happens when governments use open data from other governments.
- Business-to-Government data sharing (B2G) happens when governments use data generated by companies.
- Business-to-Business data sharing (B2B) happens when companies share data with each other.

Open data plays an important role in the first two dynamics. This chapter is mostly about the first type of data sharing, G2B, where companies consider using government-generated open data for their own business purposes.

WHAT IS OPEN DATA?

While open data has a wide range of definitions, one of the most commonly accepted (Wikipedia, n.d.) puts it this way: "Open data is the idea that some data should be freely available to everyone to use and republish as they wish, without restrictions from copyright, patents or other mechanisms of control."

The value proposition of open data is that there is much more value in sharing data than in keeping it locked up in organizations. All organizations have limited resources to create value from their own data, and opening the data up to developers, start-ups, NGOs and other organizations would multiply the resources engaged in value creation. The vision of open data is to create a thriving ecosystem around this data. McKinsey stated nearly a decade ago (Manyika et al., 2013) that open data — public information and shared data from private sources — can help create $3 trillion a year of value in seven areas of the global economy.

However, as of 2020, the value created with open data has not lived up to its promise. While there is activity, no thriving open data ecosystem has appeared in the past five years. That's probably one of the reasons the European Commission approved a new Open Data Directive (European Commission, 2019) that builds on the previous Public Sector Information Directive, last updated in 2013. The new Open Data Directive includes more compulsory data sets to be open. It also commits to creating so-called high-value data sets in areas such as Geospatial, Earth Observation and Environment, Meteorological, Statistics, Companies and Company Ownership, and Mobility.

While in principle, companies can engage with data in two different ways — consuming open data and publishing open data — in practice most companies are only considering its consumption to enrich their internal data sources.

USING OPEN DATA TO
ENRICH INTERNAL DATA

Why would companies be interested in using open data? The main reason is to enrich their internal data sources with data that helps them improve their business objectives, either for internal use cases or external data monetization. Let's see some of the benefits in more detail.

- **Data efficiency.** Data preparation and curation requires effort. Open data is published, curated data that's available for free. Therefore, if particular open data sets fit the company's needs, it may be a more efficient route to value.
- **Providing context.** Internal data sources provide, among other things, information about product and service usage. Open data might provide a wider societal and market context for better interpreting product and service use.
- **Financial efficiency.** Some open data might replace external data that's currently procured, which would imply cost savings.
- **Improving the commercial strategy.** In some countries, open data consists of thousands of rich data sets in a wide variety of subject areas. Leveraging this data in customer market research and strategic analyses can

help fine-tune a company's go-to-market strategy, planning and execution.

- **Product improvement.** Many products today use data as part of their value proposition. The inclusion of external, open data might help to improve the products.
- **Product development.** Open data might also be a source and inspiration for new products. When combined with internal data, such data-based products might enjoy a competitive advantage.

CHALLENGES WHEN USING OPEN DATA

While open data promises important benefits, there are several challenges that arise when using it for enriching internal data and supporting the business. Before companies can use open data at scale, they need to deal with these challenges in a satisfactory way. Here are some important considerations:

- **Fragmentation.** Many governments publish worldwide, or are even obliged to publish their data as open data. However, each government, regardless of whether it's a local, regional, national or international entity, can decide where to publish it. Many governments do this through a dedicated section on their website (e.g. gov. countrycode). As a result, it's hard to find specific open data sets. A company interested in open data of the country it operates in needs to look at the city, regional and national level, in addition to checking with the office of national statistics.
- **Data quality.** As with internal data, any business that wants to incorporate open data needs to trust its quality. However, it's not always clear how the data has

been generated, which forces the company to do its own quality checks.

- **Update frequency.** Many data sets become obsolete after some time. It is therefore important that the update frequency be explicitly declared, as is documenting the last time it was updated.
- **Heterogeneity.** Open data can be found in many different formats, from images, PDFs, Excel spreadsheets, CSV files and that published as linked data. For open data to work, it needs to be at least in a machine-readable format. Tim Berners Lee — the English scientist known as the creator of the World Wide Web — set up a five-start open data ranking (Lee, 2012) such that publishers can annotate their data sets with this information.
- **Lack of transparent publishing strategy.** Most governments, at all levels, decide by themselves what data to publish, without any coordination. Since there is an obligation to publish — and the KPI is about whether data has been published, not whether it's been used to create value — it is not uncommon that the published data was simply the easiest material to publish, rather than that with the most strategic value.
- **Liability.** Last, but certainly not least, there is the liability issue. When a company includes an open data feed in a consumer or a business product, what happens if the feed has problems and the customer service cannot be delivered? Who is to blame: the data provider or the company? Aspects such as data quality and update frequency are very important in this context.

POSSIBLE SOLUTIONS FOR
THE CHALLENGES OF OPEN DATA

There are several practical approaches a company can take in dealing with the challenges of open data. Let's examine them.

Niche aggregators. For the challenges related to data quality, frequency, fragmentation and heterogeneity, companies can work with so-called niche aggregators. These are usually start-ups that focus on a specific area of open data, aggregate it and then provide it for a fee, which is the basis of their business model. One successful example is Opencorporates.com, which aggregates worldwide information on corporations. TransportAPI.com aggregates all kinds of open data on transportation in the UK, and sells access to transport providers, both private and public. And, quandl.com aggregates various financial and economics open data. For companies that care more about quality and minimizing risks than free data, such aggregators offer an attractive route to enriching their internal data.

Open Data Directive. With the recently published Data Strategy of the European Commission and the new Open Data Directive of 2019, we may expect that several of the challenges mentioned above will be gradually overcome. For example, the Open Data Directive commits to publishing several high-value data sets, which will improve the publishing strategy and address the fragmentation problem.

SOME GUIDELINES FOR COMPANIES TO USE OPEN DATA

While there isn't a lot of published experience on companies using open data to enrich their internal data, I have been able to compile the following short list of common-sense guidelines:

- Open data should fulfil a defined need within the company.
- Companies that are looking to procure external data for a certain business problem should consider open data and niche aggregators.
- Before deciding to use open data, check whether it is in an appropriate format.
- Given the high variability in quality of open data, companies can benefit from a defined and approved open data inventory that only includes open data sets with sufficient credibility in terms of quality and updates.
- When companies work with third parties and vendors that make use of open data, they should require them to disclose details on data sources and licenses that apply.
- As with all data, open data must be periodically and proportionally checked for quality and fitness for purpose.
- Before open data is used in production systems, a legal risks assessment should be performed.

PUBLISHING OPEN DATA

As mentioned, most companies *use* rather than *publish* open data. Still, there are reasons why companies would publish part of their internal data as open data. Yet, rather than publishing all data in a completely open manner, they usually share it with a limited set of trusted partners.

The most frequent reason to turn to open data is to engage in 'data for good' initiatives as part of a CSR strategy. Companies could decide to publish some data sets openly for use by humanitarian organizations, to help solve important societal problems in areas such as health, climate change, hunger, poverty or inequality (see Chapter 21).

Another reason for sharing data is to enjoy the benefits of open innovation. Apart from the direct internal business needs that internal data can serve, there are many potential new business opportunities that data could help drive, and that companies themselves are not able to generate. By opening up some of their data, they can attract developers and start-ups to create new value from their internal data.

HOW SHOULD LARGE ORGANIZATIONS APPROACH OPEN DATA?

JENI TENNISON
Vice President & Chief
Strategy Adviser, The
Open Data Institute

Open data refers to data that anyone can access, use and share. People often think of open data as only coming from government, where there's a direct connection between using public resources to collect data and a responsibility to allow the public to access it. Increasingly, however, open data is also becoming an important part of the data strategies of organizations outside the public sector, including companies.

At the ODI, we work with companies and governments to build an open, trustworthy data ecosystem, where people can use data to make better decisions and manage harmful impacts. This doesn't mean we believe all data should be open, but we do think that much of the data held by organizations, including in the private sector, should be more open.

In 2020, the European Data Portal estimated that the value of open data for 'the EU28+' — the 28 European Union members, along with four free-trade partner countries — was €184 billion in 2019. That figure was forecast to reach €199-335 billion by 2025.[1]

Businesses are participating in the open data economy in different ways, including publishing open data, using it, investing in it and contributing to open data sets. The Swiss agribusiness Syngenta is publishing open data to build trust within its business ecosystem,[2] while companies like the UK health and fitness chain Everyone Active are publishing open data to improve market reach by helping potential customers find their services.[3] The media conglomerate Thomson Reuters launched PermID in 2015 to create an open persistent identifier in the finance sector, to help boost innovation.[4] Meanwhile, Facebook, Apple and Microsoft are all contributing to an openly licensed map of the world by adding data to OpenStreetMap.[5]

Working in the open to deliver equitable value from data can help large organizations like these build trust with their users and benefit from direct community feedback.

Despite this, large organizations still hoard data. A report from the Lloyd's Register Foundation[6] highlighted some of the common barriers to sharing data: concerns about commercial and legal risks, and a lack of clarity around the benefits. Frameworks to support legal, ethical and trustworthy sharing of data, such as those being developed in the EU and the UK, can help increase confidence, as can case studies that show organizations getting value from opening data, like those developed by the ODI.[7]

Open data needs to be an embedded part of the data strategy for any large organization, and geared toward enabling it to achieve its larger strategic goals, such as reaching more customers, improving supply chains, or contributing to wider societal benefits.

Enacting these strategies requires organizations to address:

- Data management processes — business policies, processes and practices that underpin data management, governance and publication.
- Knowledge and skills — steps required to create a culture of open data within an organization.
- Customer support and engagement — connection with data suppliers, data re-users and the people and communities the data is about.
- Investment and financial performance — understanding the value of their data sets, and the financial oversight and investment to support their publication.
- Strategic oversight — the strategy around data sharing and reuse, with an identified leadership with responsibility and capacity to deliver that strategy.

We have found that innovative, collaborative and imaginative leadership is the most important determinant of success. Companies need leadership that can see the strategic potential of open data, design new business models, and be willing to put the necessary investment into people, processes and technology to make it work. Those that do so unlock value, not just for themselves but for whole sectors and the wider society.

10. AI AND BIG DATA IN SMALL- AND MEDIUM-SIZED ENTERPRISES

This book is meant for large organizations and all the decisions they face when moving forward on their data and AI journey. However, in many countries, a significant part of the economy is carried by SMEs. This chapter examines how big data and AI can be used by these SMEs.

Are SMEs aware of AI and big data? Do they know what it is useful for? Are they aware of the risks? Do they have access to the right skills? What about usage in different sectors? This chapter is based on my experience teaching AI to many Spanish SMEs, as part of an ambitious program to help them in their digital transformation.[1] This was undertaken with the participation of experts from Google, eBay, Amazon, Telefónica, Salesforce and Microsoft, among others. AI is one of the 25 topics covered in the course, which is presented in more than 25 cities across Spain. Some 30 SMEs in each city have taken advantage of the course over the past three years.

In this chapter, we'll give an overview of the SME perspective on AI and big data, as well as highlight how SMEs are different from large enterprises with respect to the data and AI journey.

AN SME PERSPECTIVE ON
AI AND BIG DATA

At the start of the program, I designed a simple question-naire to get a better understanding of the state of AI and big data among SMEs in Spain. The findings are based on input from more than 50 SMEs during the first year of the course. Below we'll delve into some of the results.

Except for one, all participating SMEs had heard of AI. Asked about what they understood the term to encompass, most cited machine learning and intelligent software, fol-lowed by references to 'thinking machines' and robots. A significant percentage also felt that AI can refer to all of the above (see Figure 10.1).

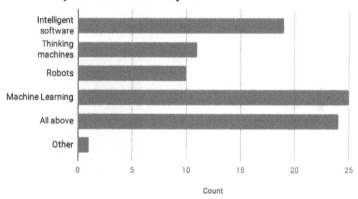

What do you understand by AI?

Figure **10.1** What do SMEs understand AI to be?

About 80% of the participants knew about AI use cases, and 75% were aware of the risks associated with this tech-nology (bias, discrimination, explainability, future of work). The majority, however, believed that the opportunities sig-nificantly outweigh the risks (Figure 10.2).

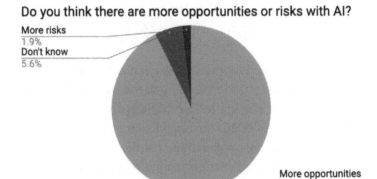

Figure 10.2 Do SMEs see more opportunities or risks associated with AI?

Most SMEs thought that AI was already here, but that much more was to come (Figure 10.3).

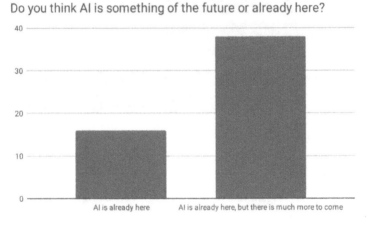

Figure 10.3 Do SMEs view AI as something of the present or the future?

However, the main challenge SMEs faced was accessing the required technical skills, such as data engineering, analytics and machine learning. More than 75% didn't have access to the right knowledge (Figure 10.4). Obviously, that hinders the uptake of AI and big data.

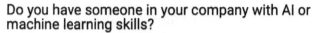

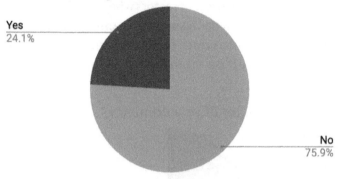

Figure 10.4 Do SMEs have profiles with knowledge of AI or machine learning?

Asked whether they were actually using AI, about 10% (6 SMEs) stated that they were. Almost 60% (31 SMEs) had plans to use it, while just over 30% (17 SMEs) reported having no current plans to use it (Figure 10.5).

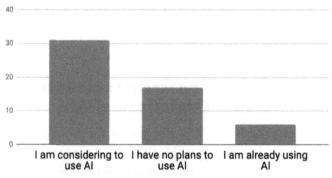

Figure 10.5 SMEs considering using AI, with no plans to do so, or actually using it

When asked what problems they've solved or plan to solve with AI, the applications they cited included predictive maintenance, sales, production, market analysis, customer care, marketing, demand prediction, robots, machine design and manufacturing, and factory optimization.

Given the large variety of sectors where SMEs are active, a broad categorization has been used, spanning services, technology, industry, consumer, food and agriculture, although almost 50% come from the industrial sector (Figure 10.6).

What is the sector of your company?

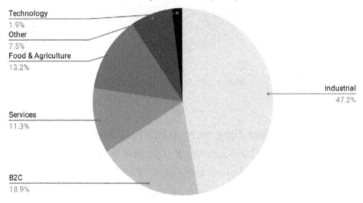

Figure 10.6 Surveyed SMEs by sector

HOW CAN SMES BENEFIT FROM BIG DATA AND AI?

AI AND DATA DIFFERENCES BETWEEN LARGE ENTERPRISES AND SMEs

To understand how SMEs can get on the AI and big data bandwagon, let's see what the differences are between large enterprises and SMEs on several dimensions relevant for AI and big data. This is explained in Table 10.1.

Dimension	Large enterprise	SME
Technology	Own IT and platforms	IT in the Cloud
	Large amount of internal data sources	Limited data sources such as Excel, web, CRM
Finance	Significant budget	Little or no budget
Business	Hundreds of possible use cases	Limited use cases around sales, marketing, operations
People	Skills and large data teams	No internal skills, no team

Table 10.1 Main differences between large enterprises and SMEs
regarding big data and AI enablement

On the technology side, as we've seen, large enterprises have their own IT and data platforms. This is in contrast to SMEs, which tend to have all or most of their IT in the cloud. Large enterprises also have hundreds of internal data sources, whereas an SME usually only has a few, such as Excel spreadsheets, data from their website and CRM material.

Regarding finance, we have seen that large enterprises spend against budgets of tens of millions of euros, whereas SMEs have very little or no budget to spend on big data and AI. And, for the little guys, making important upfront investments is also out of the question. On the business side, while large enterprises have hundreds of use cases whose value can be significant, SMEs have a much more limited set of use cases to create value from.

Finally, on the people side, we have seen that large enterprises typically have several data and AI teams, while SMEs often don't have a single person dedicated to data and AI, either due to lack of budget or because they have no access to such scarce skill profiles.

Does this mean that SMEs are excluded from the benefits of AI and big data? Not necessarily. As with many new technologies, applications are first pioneered by innovative early adopter enterprises. And then, when solutions are becoming more mature and automated, they fall within reach of smaller organizations. This is the normal new technology democratization process, and it will be no different with AI (see Chapter 17).

MINIMAL CONDITIONS FOR SMES TO APPLY DATA AND AI

There are, however, some minimal requirements for SMEs to be able to start their AI and data projects. Here are a few:

- **Access to quality data.** Without data, nothing can be done, and without quality data you can't be sure that AI or analytics generate correct recommendations or decisions. This is probably one of the most difficult thresholds to meet, not because SMEs don't possess quality data, but they often lack the technical skills necessary to access it and to check its quality. For very small enterprises, in practice, help from a technical 'friend' might solve this problem. For medium-size businesses, it might be worthwhile to subcontract just this data part to a local consultant.
- **Select the right use case.** While there are fewer potential use cases for SMEs than for large enterprises, the same criteria for selecting the best use case to start with also apply to large-, small- and medium-sized companies. Constructing an opportunity matrix based on business impact and feasibility helps prioritize use cases (see Chapter 6).
- **Analytical capability.** As we have seen in our small piece of research mentioned earlier, most SMEs have no access to data scientists. Moreover, subcontracting this kind of

capability can be expensive. Does this mean that SMEs cannot enjoy the benefits of AI? Again, not necessarily. There's a growing array of tools that provide machine learning out of the box, automating work that a data scientist would normally do. And while such tools cannot do everything a senior data scientist can, they can quite effectively cover 50-60% of it, which for an SME is usually enough. The best example of such a tool is BigML,[2] which provides a graphical drag and drop interface for conducting data science. BigML offers all popular machine-learning algorithms out of the box (see more in Chapter 17).

CONCLUSION

While big data and AI are applied much more pervasively in large enterprises, this does not mean that SMEs can't take advantage of this powerful technology. There is a growing assortment of tools that offer machine learning as a service, through intuitive graphical interfaces. They allow non-data scientists to apply, evaluate and execute machine-learning models directly on Excel spreadsheets, using data from SMEs.

TOWARD DATA LITERACY

ALBERTO TURÉGANO SCHIRMER
Partner, Líderes y Digitales

Terms such as data analytics, data science, business intelligence, big data, AI, machine learning and data storytelling are in vogue and on the lips of many. Far from being a fad, they're here to stay.

Yet, although organizations are aware of the importance of collecting, storing and processing data to turn it into useful information that improves decision-making, most are not allowing the implementation of a data-driven culture.

A recent study carried out on 65 leading firms by NewVantage Partners reveals the main causes of not being able to instill the culture of data in organizations. They are:

- People (62.5%)
- Processes (30%)
- Technology (7.5%)

There does not seem to be an overwhelming problem with technology, investment or process. In fact, there are countless technological solutions on the market that would allow organizations to extract the value that resides in data at prices that are affordable for them. What's missing are people with the necessary skills to extract and tell the stories that the data hides. There simply aren't enough analytical professionals, curious about what the data 'says,' with a hacker mentality and knowledge of analysis, data visualization or data storytelling.

We're therefore faced with a cultural problem — a problem of data literacy. This is the fundamental ability to read, work with, analyse and discuss data. Like literacy as a general concept, data literacy focuses on the competencies involved in working with data.

And how are organizations solving this problem?

Medium-sized organizations are primarily offering training and certifications for their employees. In fact, half of their budgets are being allocated to the development of skills related to the language of the data. By 2020, 80% of organizations were expected to begin deliberately developing competencies in the field of data knowledge to overcome extreme deficiencies, according to Gartner's fourth annual survey of data directors in 2019.

Smaller organizations that can't afford this investment in their employees can always be guided through their first steps by qualified consultants, who design the strategy around and train employees in the culture of data.

In any case, this is a path of no return. Data has become a strategic asset, and organizations that can treat it as such will gain a competitive advantage over the rest.

PART III

TECHNOLOGY

In the third part of this book, we will share lessons learned about decisions that relate to technology. This is not about the technology itself, but rather about the implications of corporations' technology-related decisions. These choices often have far-reaching consequences that organizations fail to anticipate.

11. CLOUD OR ON-PREMISE?

In 2008, the technology and business author Nicholas Carr published *The Big Switch* (Carr, 2008), where he envisioned that at some point in time the cloud would be similar to how we work with electricity. Namely, it's there when you need it, you plug in if you need it, and you pay for usage, with no need for large amounts of storage or computation power in your computers.

Now, 13 years later, this vision is a reality. On the consumer side, most people listen to music or watch movies in the cloud, through streaming services like Spotify or Netflix. Who is still consuming content only from a local device? Who still makes local backups of personal computers or mobile devices rather than relying on synchronized copies in the cloud? On the business side, more and more organizations are moving from on-premise infrastructure to a partial or full cloud strategy. While they still may support local software, office software like Microsoft's Office365 and Google Suite have a cloud-first orientation. If there is local usage, it is always synchronized with the cloud.

Most of us digital people know about and have experienced the general advantages of the cloud: if you lose your laptop or mobile phone, then that's *all* you've lost — only the commodity hardware. In the blink of an eye, you can recover all your data and applications from the cloud. While this chapter focuses on the use of cloud computing for AI and big data in an enterprise setting, many of these advantages also exist for other enterprise applications in the cloud.

WHY CLOUD COMPUTING FOR BIG DATA AND AI?

Let's start with arguments in favour of using enterprise cloud solutions for big data and AI.

FROM CAPEX TO OPEX

Using the cloud allows enterprises to view infrastructure as a flexible operational expenditure (Opex) rather than a capital expenditure (Capex). This avoids considerable upfront investment and allows for a 'pay as you go' approach. With little need for resources, you pay little by default and costs increase only when the business increases. While the cloud allows you to grow infrastructure (costs) in pace with the business, that doesn't mean that cloud computing is always cheaper. There are scenarios, especially in larger initiatives, where on-premise is not necessarily more expensive.

INCREASE AGILITY AND FLEXIBILITY

Who doesn't remember starting a new project and having to wait several months until the hardware had been purchased and installed? With cloud solutions, that's all ancient history. As long as you're able to pay, provisioning of infrastructure is almost instantaneous. (Of course, if you know what to buy, there's often an abundance of available services, requiring diligence in selecting the best options). Moreover, if you need more resources, either computation or storage, you can scale flexibly and pay accordingly. If you need fewer resources, scaling down is also easy and you, of course, pay less. Between 2010 and 2020, this agility and flexibility went from being an innovation to a matter of BAU.

HARD TO COMPETE WITH

The cloud giants invest billions of dollars a year in improving their cloud offering. Their pace of innovation is blistering, and they launch many new services each year. Therefore, no single company, whatever its size, is able to sustain that breakneck development, and on-premise solutions will therefore increasingly lag behind cloud offerings. This holds for functionalities that increase the speed and usefulness of the business, but also for security aspects. It is simply a matter of resources that makes it impossible for on-premise solutions to compete with the cloud.

UPDATES AND MAINTENANCE

Running big data and AI services in the cloud implies that updates and new versions are immediately available to all customers. There's no need to make it so via local updates. The same holds for corrective maintenance and restoring backups.

SECURITY

A usual argument against cloud computing is that there's a higher security risk because the data needs to leave the boundaries of the organization, and that implies loss of control. However, given the huge investments made in cloud data centres, your cloud-based data and software are probably more secure than if you maintained them on-premise. Technology-wise, the latest security-enhancing techniques will be available as soon as they are released, which is hard to achieve on-premise simply because of the economies of scale built into the hyperscale cloud providers.

While technology can solve many security risks, it cannot (yet) solve the human risk. Indeed, many security problems arise from the fact that there are people who have administrator access to software and hardware, which they need simply for maintenance reasons (upgrading software, repairing hardware, etc.). And while people get clear instructions and have to follow strict security protocols, they still make unintended mistakes, or sometimes worse. Hyperscale cloud providers utilize automated processes, using AI and robotics, to an extreme degree, with hardly any human involvement in administration tasks. Automation to this extent is not feasible for on-premise situations simply because organizations lack the scale to make the required investments worthwhile. In fact, in many situations the human is the weakest security link in the loop.

IAAS, PAAS, MLAAS FOR AI

There are different offerings in the cloud related to AI and big data. The most basic one is Infrastructure as a Service (IaaS). This means you use the cloud as an external resource for storage and computation, but you're in control of your own computation stack. The next level up is to use the cloud as a platform — Platform as a Service (PaaS) — with specific big data and AI facilities residing on top of basic storage and computation. Google's service includes its popular TensorFlow and BigQuery. Microsoft's Azure includes its Cognitive Services, databases, machine learning tools, etc. Likewise, Amazon provides a variety of services related to data management and machine-learning. The advantage of PaaS is the availability of building blocks that relieve developers from having to piece together basic things, so they can focus on value creation. The inherent disadvantage is the lock-in such platforms create. Once started with one of the big hyperscale players, it becomes harder to move to another provider.

A new cloud trend is out-of-the-box machine learning as a service (MLaaS). This frees users from the details of data and algorithms and lets them directly focus on applications. BigML is one of those providers. The only thing a user needs is data, which is uploaded to the cloud and will be checked for quality. The user can select from many different machine-learning models (both supervised and unsupervised), train and evaluate the models, and if successful put them into operation. Such tools really democratize machine-learning capabilities beyond data scientists and other technical profiles, putting them into the hands of business people (see Chapter 17).

WHY STAY ON-PREMISE?

Even with all these advantages, there are still organizations that prefer to run their AI and big data systems on-site. One reason is that some organizations feel on-premise is safer because it all stays within the company's control, and all security measures are under the direct responsibility of the in-house team. Still, as we've said, it is unlikely that any individual organization can keep up with the security efforts of the hyperscale cloud providers. Another often-heard explanation for keeping it all in-house is that regulations prevent companies from using the cloud. But, that doesn't hold. I've heard companies cite supposed regulatory prohibitions, and there was always another company in the same sector that did use the cloud. Staying on-premise, therefore, is more often related to a 'feeling' of security than to real security.

While there seem to be very few reasons for not moving to the cloud, there *are* some additional factors worthwhile for consideration before taking a final decision. First, software running in the cloud is often closely integrated with software running in-house. This implies that new versions and updates need to be coordinated for business continuity reasons. As such, cloud providers need to inform their customers of upcoming updates and give them a period of time to adapt. Large organizations typically require significant time to plan for such updates, while cloud providers prefer to run the latest versions of their software. For large organizations, it's therefore important to be aware of the update policies of their cloud providers. Some providers hardly give any notice and time to adapt, while others are more business-friendly and sometimes — particularly with large multinational customers — even negotiate personalized terms and conditions.

There are also some macro-arguments against the use of hyperscale cloud providers. For instance, they've been accused of forming an oligopoly. In 2018, the two largest cloud players in the world, Amazon AWS and Microsoft Azure, controlled almost 50% of the market, while the top four, additionally including Google and Alibaba, controlled 60% (DZone, 2020). And, consider that Google and Microsoft are growing at an annual rate of more than 50%. One risk this presents is the prospect of a single point of catastrophic failure. If Amazon AWS, for whatever reason, were down for some time, it would have a significant impact on the global economy. Another consequence is the enormous concentration of economic power in a very few companies. If most of the world's business is run on the machines of fewer than five cloud providers, these five players hold extraordinary power.

DIFFERENT CLOUD STRATEGIES

PURE PLAY STRATEGIES

There are different strategies for using the cloud for AI and big data. A pure play strategy means that all storage and computation is happening in the cloud, and that little or nothing is happening on-premise. This is a popular approach for SMEs, and for newly created companies. An advantage of a pure cloud strategy is that you can use one of the providers' PaaS offerings in big data and machine learning, which prevents an organization from installing AI- and big data-specific software on-premise.

The opposite strategy is not to use the cloud at all, and do all storage and computation on-premise. While a full in-house approach for AI and big data is seen less frequently, it still happens with large organizations that defined their strategy many years ago. They generally have significant storage and computation resources at their disposal, which are sufficient to support their AI and big data initiatives.

HYBRID CLOUD STRATEGIES

A hybrid strategy implies a mixture of cloud and on-premise. One approach is that certain processes always run on-premise while others are always in the cloud. Another possibility is that processes always start on-premise, and additional required capacity is then moved to the cloud. A typical case in AI is to run deep-learning training sessions in the cloud because of the huge capacity they may need. While running such processes on-premise might take weeks, the scalability of the cloud may reduce the required time significantly.

For organizations that still worry about putting personal data in the cloud, there exists a privacy-related best practice for a hybrid cloud strategy based on pseudonymization.

While personal data is often needed when a machine-learning model is run in operation — to reach a particular customer, for example — anonymized or pseudonymized data is often sufficient for training the model. In this best practice, the data set that contains personal (customer) data remains on premise, and before it's uploaded to the cloud, all data is anonymized/pseudonymized. The machine-learning process takes place on this anonymous/pseudonymous data and identifies clusters of customers based on specific attributes. Once the model is finished, it is then run on-premise with specific customers. As an example, consider the business problem of customer churn: customers who voluntarily leave the brand. With historical data on customers who either left or stayed, it's possible to machine learn what specific characteristics predict those who will leave or remain loyal to the company. To learn those characteristics, there is no need for personal data, and the machine-learning process runs in the cloud. For retaining specific customers, though, personal data is needed, which happens on-premise.

CONCLUSION

We have seen several arguments for and against using the cloud for AI and big data. But what does this mean for specific organizations? In general, for historical reasons, large organizations already have on-premise infrastructure in place, so it wouldn't make sense to use a pure cloud strategy, if only for amortizing the investments made in this infrastructure. However, since AI and big data might be a new area for a company, and if current on-premise infrastructure is already heavily used by traditional IT systems, there might be an opportunity to use a pure cloud strategy for AI and big data. As mentioned, there's still much development to be done in this field, so agility is key. If your on-premise infrastructure is optimized for managing the operation of traditional systems (billing, HR, service activation, etc.), it is likely to have rigid processes. If so, you might prefer to move directly to the cloud. If you can't — for example, if your organization doesn't allow you to use the cloud for AI and big data — you could consider Gartner's bimodal approach (Mariani, 2019), which defines two modes of IT that operate in parallel. The first one is traditional, emphasizing scalability, efficiency, safety and accuracy. The second is nonsequential, emphasizing agility, interactivity and speed (see also Chapter 2).

DATA ON-PREMISE VERSUS DATA
IN THE PUBLIC CLOUD

**JOSÉ LUIS
AGÚNDEZ**
Group VP, Head of
Data Architecture,
Banco Santander

Moving your data to a public cloud infrastructure is a deeply scary move. But, the promise of huge savings in IT spending, and ease of operation, are very powerful reasons to consider it.

Most of the public cloud benefits come from the flexibility of automatically growing or shrinking the IT resources (e.g. web portal servers, data storage, etc.) required to meet business demands, such as Black Friday sales. All this, without the need to plan weeks or months ahead, purchase and install IT equipment, and after the peak demand watch it lay idle while you pay good money to keep the lights on. It's simply pay-as-you-go, with your credit card.

So, then, why do many companies still not adopt the cloud?

One challenge for many facing this decision is that they were in business well before the 'digital native' wave. Or, even in newer companies, their IT staff might not be comfortable when infrastructure services are managed by others.

Many businesses start with innovation projects in the public cloud, as a way to understand and prepare for the bigger endeavour of moving other workloads there. As a result, IT teams get comfortable with a 'lift and shift' approach, replacing IT hardware in a data centre for the equivalent virtual hardware in the cloud. However, this move to cloud Infrastructure as a Service (IaaS), does not provide flexible resources. It merely replaces physical with *virtual machines*, and extends the data centre with a new, remote location. Yet, basically nothing changes, as the data never leaves the company's data centre perimeter. With cloud IaaS, the benefits of automatic scaling of IT resources are never realized.

However, the only way to achieve all the benefits is to fully embrace the cloud Platform as a Service (PaaS).

The challenge with cloud PaaS is that the data must be uploaded to the public cloud. Wow. Now, the company's IT staff needs to embark on a journey of discovery of a completely new platform full of unfamiliar services for everything from networking and security to data ingestion, and all the way to data visualization with your customers' data on it. It can be quite an IT roller-coaster ride.

In any journey, having a map and some reliable information about the places you're going to travel to is a valuable asset. So, let's try to provide some context, as part of the journey's anticipation and preparation:

- **Cybersecurity.** I cannot emphasize this enough: make sure to get the most experienced talent you can in this area, because cloud security is going to be a BIG DEAL during your journey. You will need a lot of this talent to build trust in the new platform. Execute cybersecurity poorly and you'll be stuck forever in approval processes where no one wants to sign off. Or, even worse, things are approved and they go very badly, as in a data breach type of crisis (Shu et al., 2017).
- **Legal and Compliance.** For non-technical teams in charge of protecting the company, the cloud is a completely new frontier full of geo-political and legal barriers to entry. Their concerns about unknown legal actions, regulator fines, etc., are very real, and can affect both the financial bottom line and the company's brand reputation.
- **Start with a few, small wins.** Think carefully about which IT systems to migrate to the cloud, obviously avoiding those used to run the business. A safe start would involve the business intelligence and other analytical and reporting functions.
- **Team re-skilling.** The cultural change will take years, so get everyone familiarized with the new services, and then go deep

into the specific aspects needed by different teams (developers, operations, data, etc.).

Meanwhile, some companies are using the cloud indirectly, via managed services, when a service provider (Salesforce, Workday, etc.) has its IT hosted in the cloud. With this Software as a Service (SaaS) model, benefits of public cloud are experienced by the service provider, while the client company might use service level agreements to try to contractually ensure its requirements.

So, as you complete the cloud journey, make sure to add SaaS to your cloud success metrics!

12. LOCAL OR GLOBAL STORAGE? UNIFIED DATA MODEL OR NOT?

Apart from the decision about cloud or on-premise, as discussed in the previous chapter, another important big data decision large (particularly international) organizations have to make is whether they store the data locally, in the businesses, or in a centrally-controlled headquarters server, and whether to use a unified data model or not. These are important decisions because of their significant impact on how data-related assets are managed and how the costs are assigned to different parts of the organization.

RELEVANT CONCEPTS

In order to understand the factors influencing these decisions, it's important to define some relevant concepts, such as local versus global storage and the type of data model.

LOCAL OR GLOBAL STORAGE

For a multinational organization it is important to decide where data is physically stored. Will it be stored at headquarters, or at each local or geographical business, or will it be a mix of those? Global data storage does not necessarily imply control over the data. It can be physically stored in one specific place, but control and access can still be managed by the local businesses. This decision does, however, have an important influence on the cost model, potential synergies, coordination of progress and building up the required skills.

UNIFIED DATA MODEL OR NOT

This concept is related to the format and semantics of the data stored across an organization. Very few non-native digital organizations will have a unified data model spanning their organization. A unified model allows for easy comparison and combining of data, and allows for lifting and shifting of applications across different businesses. Building a unified data model is, however, a complex and slow process.

DIFFERENT PRACTICAL SCENARIOS FOR STORAGE AND DATA MODEL

So, how should large organizations go about making those decisions? In this section, we will explain different scenarios, along with their advantages and disadvantages. The scenarios are anchored in typical organizational realities, such as decentralized organizations where power sits in the operating businesses, versus centralized organizations where power is mostly concentrated in headquarters. Of course, most companies operate somewhere between these extremes, but it is important to take into account where the emphasis lies. We'll also discuss some typical intermediate models. We will see that a 'correct' decision strongly relates with the data maturity of the organization. In my experience, many multinationals behave like a pendulum when it comes to de/centralization, where every so many years (typically 5-7) the model changes.

Generally speaking, advantages of a centralized organizational model include better strategic alignment between the local businesses, and synergies in terms of costs, skills and markets. General disadvantages of a centralized model include slow decision-making because decisions need to be aligned with headquarters. As a consequence, a centralized model implies less autonomy for local businesses.

I believe that after many years of following one specific model (centralized or decentralized), people will have had enough of managing all the disadvantages inherent to the specific model in their day-to-day business. And then, the advantages of the other model become increasingly attractive. When the change happens, people are happy that the disadvantages have disappeared, enjoy the advantages, and plan to properly manage the 'new' inherent disadvantages. However, after several years, the advantages become the 'normal' way and the disadvantages get more weighty. They eventually become so strong that a change is again provoked, leading to a move back to the previous model, possibly in an evolved manner.

THE DECENTRALIZED ORGANIZATION – LOCAL STORAGE, LOCAL DATA MODEL

Many large, global corporations have grown through acquisitions of local businesses in their sector. Such multinationals are inherently decentralized, although there may be many corporate attempts to craft a more centralized operation and culture. As far as data is concerned, each local operation in such organizations usually has its own data platform (a data warehouse or big data platform) that it manages autonomously. Such a data platform can run on-premise or in the cloud, can be operated internally or outsourced, and it usually has a data model fully defined by, and fitting the needs of, the local business.

Those types of organizations can still have global programs to coordinate the data strategy, in terms of sharing best practices and use cases, and can even have a kind of global committee for organizing this. Yet, when it comes to data storage and execution of use cases, each local business is in charge.

The advantages of such a local organization include:

- The speed of action is fully determined by the priorities of the local business. No coordination or permission is required from headquarters.
- Local businesses are in control and feel empowered. This is important for accountability reasons — success and failure are felt as direct consequences of local business actions. There's also a motivational reason, because a decentralized model promotes proactive actions from the local business.
- On the operational side, the latency (speed) of access to the data is determined by the local business.

The disadvantages of a fully decentralized organization include:

- It is no small matter to try and aggregate data and insights from the local businesses at the global corporate level, since each local business has its own data model (format and definitions) and platforms.
- Sharing use cases from one operation to another provides limited savings. While the experience can be shared in terms of best practices, lifting and shifting the solution is almost impossible due to the heterogeneity of the data. It's common knowledge that in the implementation of big data use cases the majority of the effort is spent on obtaining, understanding and cleansing the data and much less is spent on the analytics itself: in the range of 70% on data and 30% on analytics. Since, in a decentralized model, each local business has its own

data model, the data effort is still needed for implementing each use case.

- The decentralized model only allows for small synergies in terms of costs. Since each local business is autonomous in deciding what data platform to use, there is little to leverage the global scale to develop common requirements and negotiate better contracts.

In terms of the data maturity of organizations, the decentralized model works best for those in an early phase of the data transformation journey. They don't yet have valuable experience that can be shared across the group. A decentralized model allows for bottom-up experimentation, where each local business gains important experience. Once some experience is gathered, it starts to make sense to share best- and not-so-good-practices. Psychologically, it's also easier to accept guidance from others if they are perceived to have concrete experience and good results. It's also easier to accept guidance if you have experienced specific, tangible problems.

The risk of immature companies taking a decentralized approach too early on is that a lot of effort and investments are steered in a specific direction that may sound good on paper, but in practice might not be workable. This is one of the risks of working from the start with external consultants, who are sometimes overly eager to sell a specific approach that worked successfully in another client organization (see Chapter 15).

THE CENTRALIZED ORGANIZATION – CENTRAL STORAGE, UNIFIED DATA MODEL

Not surprisingly, the opposite applies in a centralized organization. In a fully centralized organization, all important data is stored in a central data lake or big data platform and complies with a centrally defined data model. Central data storage allows for a coordinated approach in terms of platform, tools, operations, team and skills, etc. A unified data model allows for the fast, easy combination of data coming from different operations and businesses, to seamlessly integrate without extra effort.

Many of the disadvantages of a decentralized organization are in fact advantageous in a centralized approach:

- It is easy to aggregate insights and data from local operations into a group-wide corporate overview.
- Sharing use cases from one local business to another is almost instantaneous, since both the data and the analytics part can be transferred as is.
- Significant synergies (in costs and skills) can be obtained because there is only one physical platform managed by one team or provider.

Similarly, the advantages of a decentralized approach become disadvantages to be managed in a centralized approach:

- Local operational decisions take longer (i.e. more red tape and bureaucracy) because several operational activities go through the central operations team.
- Investments and other important decisions need to be approved by headquarters for compliance with the corporate strategy.
- Visible costs for big data at headquarters increase due to central management and operation.
- Speed of access to the platform might be impacted in certain parts of the business that are physically far away from headquarters, due to the varying reliability of internet connectivity.

The centralized model works fine for organizations with relatively high data maturity. Designing and maintaining a unified data model across different geographical businesses is not an easy task. If not managed correctly, this can turn into a nightmare for both headquarters and local businesses. A central platform for all data means highly visible costs at the corporate level, which only data-mature companies can afford. In these companies, the value of data is not questioned, and costs are seen as a profitable investment. The high visible costs will scare less data-mature organizations, and with the first calls for cost reduction the project's ambitions will likely be scaled down to a minimum, before it's finally killed. All in all, it will have been a waste of time for everybody.

The decision for a de/centralized approach is, of course, not a binary one. There are many approaches in between the extremes. We will discuss two of the most common ones.

THE TRANSFORMING ORGANIZATION

Two examples that are situated between the extremes are organizations that have chosen for a unified data model with local storage, and those that use central storage, but with a free data model.

GLOBAL STORAGE, LOCAL DATA MODEL

This model is appropriate for organizations that have a strong IT area, or that have just started their investment in data, and where headquarters wants to promote big data initiatives in the local operating businesses. In this model, headquarters provides all interested local businesses with access to a central big data platform with tools, where they can store and access data and run analytics. The local business can store the data as they have it, as there's no need to comply with a corporate unified data model. The advantage of this approach is that it lowers the entry barrier for businesses to start, because data expertise, platform procurement, privacy and security are dealt with by headquarters.

Depending on the funding model, use of the central data platform might be free, for a calculated fee or based on actual use. One of the associated disadvantages is that businesses start to store data for the sake of storing it, without specific business use cases in mind (see Chapter 6). This is, of course, not ideal, but having such a central platform in place definitely lowers the barrier to start playing around with data. Another disadvantage is that the costs become very visible at headquarters, and might start to raise questions among financial people. Yet, in terms of the data journey, it is also an advantage that the costs are explicitly known.

Having data of all local businesses centrally available also has the theoretical advantage of facilitating 'global' analytics across the whole organization. After all, all data sits in the same physical platform. However, this is only possible if a unified data model is available. Moreover, for privacy reasons (e.g., GDPR in Europe), in case the data is personal data, cross analyses or data sharing are not allowed between local businesses without explicit customer consent. However, such sharing and analysis at the central platform are allowed when data is anonymized before it's uploaded to the central platform. Also for security and privacy reasons, this is a privacy-enhancing best practice when storing data externally (see Chapter 11).

A central big data platform is usually centrally provided and maintained, either by an in-house team, outsourced to a vendor, or by a combination of both. In any case, such platforms are managed and evolved through a central road map that needs to balance the requirements of the different local businesses. I've found that this is not always easy, because local businesses might operate in different markets that require different features from the big data platform. Therefore, it's not uncommon to end up with many platform features on the road map, increasing the cost and delaying the less prioritized features for delivery. This will obviously lead to complaints by the businesses that requested those features. Another complication associated with this approach is the need for complex version management, as different businesses may run different versions of the platform that need to be centrally maintained. Releases are planned based on matching overall priorities with available budget. Indeed, experience teaches that it is hard to keep all businesses happy at the same time.

One possible solution is to let the local business that really needs a certain feature pay for its development. This will fast-track the feature on the development road map, making it available in the next release. Once available, it is also available for other local businesses. The 'paying' business is served, and thus happy, while other local businesses have also gotten access to the feature, even though it was not their priority.

Another possible problem with this approach is that local businesses do not like to depend on a global road map managed by headquarters, claiming that their market is very specific and the central solution isn't appropriate. Sometimes this concern is rooted in technical issues, such as inadequate latency of access to the central platform, but sometimes it reflects a more emotional aspect of not wanting to depend on headquarters for business results. A possible solution is that by default all business follow the corporate strategy of the central platform, but if local businesses have real problems with this, they can escalate it to the Executive Committee and defend their preference. If so authorized, the local business can then go its own way; if not, it has to comply with the corporate data strategy. A separate problem, with likely the same type of solution, is when a local business already had a local big data platform in place when the central platform was created, and prefers to continue working locally to amortize its investment.

LOCAL STORAGE, UNIFIED DATA MODEL

The final approach we'll discuss is to have data stored locally in the business (on-premise or in the cloud), but a common data model, with shared definitions and semantics, agreed upon between headquarters and all businesses. Headquarters and the local businesses would come to an agreement on what to include and not include in the data model. A unified model defines all concepts, attributes and possible values. The two extremes of an agreed model involve the **intersection** (only defining what's common to all businesses) and the **union** of the local data models (including everything used by any of the local businesses). Reality usually sits somewhere in between. The intersection is usually not expressive enough to cover all business needs, while the union is usually redundant and makes the unified model too big and unmanageable. A good approach would be to start with the intersection and then gradually include additional concepts that are justified by the different local businesses. This at least guarantees that different concepts with the same meaning end up as one concept.

There are plenty of advantages to using such a unified data model across a multinational organization, which have already been mentioned as benefits of a centralized data approach. It is easier to transfer successful use cases from one local business to another due to the saved effort on data integration. Also, global insights across the different businesses are possible due to the standardized model — for example, the definition of an 'active customer' is the same across all businesses. And, the fact that storage and access remain under local control implies that local businesses remain autonomous for an important part of data management.

There are, of course, also several challenges related to a unified data model. For one, there may not be agreement across the business that a unified model is needed.

This sort of proposal usually comes from headquarters, and local businesses must be convinced and buy in to the idea. Naturally, local businesses prefer to remain in charge of their data strategy, and centralization interferes with this notion. Therefore, organizations should expect some initial resistance to a centralized data approach. A lot of tact and clever evangelizing is needed to get all businesses on board. One tactic that might work is to create incentives to join the unified approach. For example, local businesses that adopt the unified model could be able to reuse analytical use cases that only work with the unified data model. Businesses complying with the data model would be entitled to use the code and algorithms for free, while these that don't adopt it will not have access to those assets. (Their data model is not compatible anyway).

Once local businesses agree on the need to adopt the unified data model, and decide to apply it, a complex migration process starts. Indeed, the transition from a local data model to a unified, corporate one is not trivial, and it may be too complex to perform in a short period. An alternative approach would be that local businesses have a dual policy: they maintain their local data model to run most of their business as usual, but for new applications and analyses they use the unified model by exposing or publishing their local data model in terms of the unified one. If successful, over time, when all content is available in the new data model, the local model can be shut down and BAU can happen through the unified data model.

Another challenge of a unified data model is its evolution and corresponding version management. It is clear that a data model is not fixed, and evolves according to business in an evolving market. So, while it's already a challenge to define the first version of the unified data model, new complexities are introduced when it evolves. Some specific local business may need a new data concept, which it can propose to the central team running the unified data model. This team will then evaluate whether this new data concept is justified, and if so they'll include it in the central data model, resulting in a new version. This new version is then given to the local business that requested it. However, you'll now have one local business with a new version, whereas the rest of the businesses are still using the original version. One can imagine that this requires a complex process of version management, updates and maintenance of certain previous versions. In essence, this is not any different than the management of software updates, but it's something that requires much dedication. Otherwise, things will spiral out of control.

A final disadvantage of this model is that agreeing upon, defining and implementing a unified data model requires time, during which resources need to be dedicated that cannot be applied to more short-term objectives. For a multinational organization operating in more than ten geographies, you should think about committing a few years for the full process. This obviously requires a good deal of organizational patience.

For all these reasons, a unified data model is typically most suitable for data-mature organizations that have several years of experience with big data. Trying to apply this approach from the start of the data journey will likely result in failure because of low buy-in from the local businesses. In the initial transformation phase, businesses like to explore with data, to better understand its value, but also to quickly understand specific challenges. Forcing a unified data model in this phase is likely to be counterproductive. Moreover, if asked why a unified data model does work for more mature organizations, the answer is likely that they've suffered the consequences of not having a unified model, and that 'suffering' helps demonstrate the value of the effort.

CONCLUSION

Observing and learning from the experience of different organizations, we can conclude that multinationals just starting their data and AI journey tend to experiment locally, using their own data models and local storage solutions. More mature organizations tend to move toward more globally unified solutions, because they have suffered the consequences of a fully local approach. There are, of course, exceptions; some organizations have jumped directly to a global approach. This doesn't mean that they'll fail, but those organizations have to be extra aware of the challenges they face and manage them properly.

So, if you are a multinational corporation about to start the data and AI journey, what is the optimal data storage model? Based on my experience, I would say:

- Do local experiments (i.e. different local businesses try different approaches).
- Identify best practices.
- Generalize the best practices into a global approach to be applied across the group. Notice that a best practice may refer to both a local and global solution.
- Manage centrally-driven initiatives as assets with processes and resources.

Of course, many organizations today won't find themselves in such a situation because they've already made some progress on their data and AI journey (maybe not taking all decisions explicitly). They still can learn much from the experience of others, as described in this chapter.

THE VALUE OF THE QUALITY OF DATA

**FRANCISCO
JOSÉ MONTALVO**
Chief Data Officer,
Telefónica

We have read quite a few of times that if you want to do AI properly, you need tons of data. This is true, isn't it? However, it is not common to find a correlation between the quality of the service provided by such AI and the quality of the data used for its training. In environments where information is coming from a vast array of very different systems, entailing different technical approaches and with different SLAs, it becomes necessary to ensure consistency, coherence and measurable quality.

At Telefónica, we decided to face the problem starting from the ground up, with a common dictionary of data that was designed from scratch. This helps ensure that the same reality is always described in the same way. The dictionary, called the Unified Reference Model (URM), comprises a number of categories: customer, traffic, network, enterprise, platform, insights, etc., across a number of entities (400+ and counting). The corresponding variables (6,000+) describe in detail every angle of the business and the possible combinations.

Through the combination of a minimum number of entities, we are able to build the reality, with a level of detail that depends on the specific need. For analytical purposes, aggregated information considering specific time frames and clusters of interest will work. If we're planning to use a machine-learning product for characterization and personalization, the number of entities and variables will grow significantly, with special focus on getting enough history to ensure proper training. And, when using deep learning, we will likely use a significant part of the total available data to make the neural networks learn efficiently, flagging failed attempts and focusing on improving the quality of the results generated.

However, in all the cases, quality of data will be described through its metadata, providing the algorithm with the information required to achieve the best possible outcome. URM supports batch and real-time data, satisfying depth and latency needs. Evolution toward URM is possible because the management of data is evolving from human-driven to a system-driven approach. Data quality is analysed every time the data set is ingested in the AI platform, metadata is attached for its detailed description, and every algorithm is aware of which data is available, how often and with what degree of minimum quality.

Migration to a fully URM-empowered model is a multi-year effort, being paid for through the creation of complex AI products that could not otherwise exist in our company.

13. WHERE TO RUN THE ANALYTICS

In previous chapters, we have discussed the decisions related to where and how data can be stored and managed: locally or centrally, and with a free or unified data model. Similar decisions need to be taken with respect to the analytics run on top of the data. Should analytics be run at headquarters or by local businesses? Should it be run by the data team or by the various business units?

In this chapter, we will discuss the pros and cons of the different options and relate those decisions to the different stages of the data journey. As you will notice, the central versus local analytics discussion is similar to that for data. However, there are also differences: while the analytics function can be moved around between departments, the data function always needs some notion of centralization because there should only be a single source of the 'truth' within an organization. If the data function is spread out between different departments or businesses, there's significant danger that different businesses will work with different data, increasing the risk of inconsistent conclusions based on data.

DEFINING THE CONCEPTS

Before discussing this further, we need to define some relevant concepts. First of all — and we assume most readers will be familiar with this — we distinguish between data and analytics. Data is the material representing the facts and situation in the real world, relative to a certain (business) problem. Analytics is the process, tasks, algorithms, activities, etc., that are run on top of the data to either describe or analyse the current situation, predict what will happen, or prescribe what actions to perform in the future. Data and analytics are therefore closely related, and they form part of the same value chain. There is no analytics without data, and data without analytics does not create value.

For multinational corporations, there are two levels where these decisions are relevant:

- At the group level, whether analytics are run at headquarters or at the local operating businesses.
- At the level of each operating business, whether analytics are run centrally or by each business unit.

It is important to keep these two levels in mind when reviewing the situation in your organization, as illustrated in Figure 13.1. While the arguments in favour or against are similar regardless of the level, the importance of the arguments for the corresponding decisions may be different.

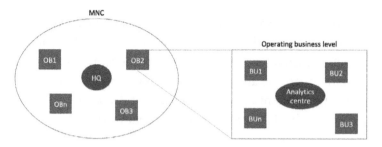

Figure 13.1 Two levels of organization for the analytics decision
OB stands for Operating Business, and BU for Business Unit

THE IMPORTANT DECISIONS TO TAKE

Given these concepts, the important decisions regarding analytics are the following:

- Does the organization create a global centre of excellence serving headquarters (HQ) as well as the operating businesses? Or, does each operating business have full responsibility for the analytics function? See the left part of Figure 13.1.
- Within each operating business, is there a central analytics department, such as a centre of excellence, that serves all business units? Or, does each unit have its own dedicated analytics function? See the right part of Figure 13.1.

These decisions represent extremes; the reality generally lies somewhere in between. For instance, HQ may have a coordinating function in terms of the analytics methodology, tools and software, while the operating businesses execute the analytics tasks. Or, HQ may take care of the analytical use cases that have a global, cross-market scope (i.e. are implemented across all operating businesses), while each operating business takes care of the analytical use cases specifically applicable to the local market.

Another relevant decision point is whether the analytics mission is part of the data function, or a separate functional group (see Chapter 3). As we will see in the remainder of this chapter, there are advantages and disadvantages associated with the different options, and the best decisions are often related to the data maturity of the organization.

THE CENTRE OF EXCELLENCE APPROACH

Many large corporations start their data and AI journey by setting up an analytics centre of excellence. Such an entity implies the creation of a specialized group of analytics and machine-learning experts in charge of creating value from data. In the ideal situation, an analytics centre of excellence enjoys the support of top management and has an allocated annual budget, making it a realistic approach to putting data and analytics on the company's road map. It is not uncommon for companies to aggressively recruit analytics leaders from the market to infuse a centre of excellence with experience and credibility from the beginning. A centre of excellence usually sets up and leads all analytics projects in a company, with the mission to demonstrate and realize the economic value of data and analytics for the organization. The centre of excellence works with the different operating businesses or business units to solve business problems using data analytics.

Depending on data maturity and on how it is organized, such centres of excellence can focus on the analytics or machine learning part only, or might also need to take care of getting access to quality data. In more mature organizations, there's usually a specific data organization (e.g. a CDO area that takes care of data access and quality). However, at the start of an organization's data journey, the analytics centre often needs to take care of the full data value chain.

It is important that decision-makers are aware of this, because highly paid analytical experts (data scientists) might get frustrated by having to deal too much with data engineering rather than with analytics. Managers often confuse data engineering and data science (analytics) and consider them synonyms, but that is an error that might undermine their data strategy. One of the best practices around analytics centres of excellence is that they not only consider data science, but also data engineering, incorporating both technical profiles.

As discussed in the previous section, in multinationals, a centre of excellence can be applied at two levels (see Figure 13.1): at the group level (HQ) and at the operating business level. The considerations mentioned above apply to both levels.

There are several advantages to implementing an analytics centre of excellence:

- It pulls together scarce data profiles in one place and gives them importance. This is valuable for the business, which receives a message that analytics is important. It's also significant for the employees of the centre: it makes them feel that they belong to a key new initiative where they can shine and have impact, which greatly stimulates motivation.
- By pulling all analytics activities together, it's easier to create critical mass and thus achieve tangible results in a short time frame, which is essential to maintain momentum across the organization. An analytics centre of excellence doesn't come for free, and other businesses might envy and therefore question the necessary investments. Showing tangible results is the best way to overcome such obstacles.
- Having all the technical people together in a unit dramatically accelerates the learning process of all involved. Rather than having individuals dispersed across the

organization, each trying to address difficult problems through their personal networks, having them all in one place facilitates asking questions about tough technical problems. It also prompts people to challenge each other, and ultimately create better technical solutions.

- An analytics centre of excellence is attractive for future team members, as it shows the organization's commitment to data and AI. This is especially important as hiring talent in this space can be challenging.
- It is relatively easy to work on strategic initiatives that have no direct short-term application to a specific business need.
- The central budget dedicated to the analytics centre of excellence makes explicit what the organization is investing in analytics, allowing it to make better decisions in terms of what investment is reasonable for obtaining results.

These advantages do not come for free, and bring distinct disadvantages that need to be managed properly:
- To some extent, it's important to let the analytics centre of excellence establish itself and allow it to explore and discover opportunities with data and analytics. This creates knowledge and experience that later can be applied to business problems. However, care should be taken to not create an isolated unit that's detached from the business. Experience shows that this is a real risk, and business units might view the centre as a group of technical geeks doing fun stuff but not tackling business needs. One way to mitigate this risk is to install a specific role that connects the analytics expertise with specific business needs. Those roles are referred to as data translators, engagement teams or business partners. They can be organized by geography, use cases or priorities.

- An analytics centre of excellence has to serve the needs of the different business units. When data and analytics has become BAU — it's now the normal way of operating — there's a risk of the centre turning into a bottleneck. After all, it has a limited amount of resources and people. If there is more demand than capacity, prioritization will be necessary, which might create tension between the centre and some unserved businesses. This needs to be carefully managed. One approach might be to create a cross-company analytics or data board with representatives from all business units, with an emphasis on transparent decision-making.
- While we've seen that it can be an advantage to know the cost of establishing the analytics centre, it might also be a risk. When visible results are lacking, the company may start to wonder whether there will be sufficient return on investment. As mentioned in Chapter 8, experience tells us that 18-24 months is the maximum period for achieving tangible financial results. Any centre of excellence should therefore be managed in a way that delivers such results before that deadline. One way of achieving that is by selecting the right use cases to work on, as discussed in Chapter 6.

A centre of excellence makes sense when companies have detected data and AI activity in their local businesses or business units, and they realize there's a lot of duplication of activities and errors, and a lack of a common approach. But, as we've seen, a centre of excellence requires investment and therefore top management endorsement and support.

THE LOCAL APPROACH

In the local approach to analytics and AI, the analytical and machine-learning capacity sits in the operating businesses and/or in the business units. This is often the case before an organization has explicitly decided to formulate a data and AI strategy from headquarters. Even before data and AI is recognized as an important part of the digital transformation strategy, it's likely that there will be several data and AI champions in the different units who saw an opportunity in data and who've started their own initiatives in the area, leveraging their own resources. Those initiatives can have more or less visibility, depending on the champion leading the initiative. Vocal champions will be instrumental in getting data and AI on top management's radar.

The advantages of a local model are clear:

- This approach is close to the business. That is, all initiatives are business-driven and try to solve a real business problem. This is in contrast to a centre of excellence approach, where sometimes initiatives are more technology driven.
- Since the analytics is run for and by the business, the speed is fully determined by the business itself. If it solves an important, urgent problem, more resources can and will be dedicated.
- The fact that an analytics team (even if small) has been set up locally empowers the local business, which drives accountability.
- Given that all investments are local and coming from existing, approved budgets, it is unlikely that some business will complain about the company's investment in data and AI.

Having said that, the disadvantages are also not surprising:

- There is little organizational learning, as each analytics area operates in isolation without connecting to a wider community. This leads to repeating errors in different parts of the organization. Also, there's little opportunity to learn from peers, leading to slower progress and little accumulation of experience.

- There can be duplication of effort and investment. When several local initiatives happen in parallel, there is a risk of buying the same license several times, missing negotiation power with providers, acquisition of similar data or AI platforms, etc.

- Attracting data and AI talent is not only a matter of having the budget to do so. It is also about offering a stimulating and motivating environment for such specialized professionals. I've heard several times that such people do not come only for the salary, but mostly for the challenge of working with complex, exciting data. Data scientists, AI engineers and data engineers are scarce resources who can choose between many different opportunities. For all these reasons, it is hard for local analytics teams to attract top talent.

- Most data and AI applications respond directly to concrete business needs. It's therefore difficult to perform strategic activities that might have an important impact in the longer term, leading to missed opportunities for the future.

A TYPICAL OR IDEAL SCENARIO RELATED TO DATA MATURITY

Every organization is different, and it is therefore impossible to define a single approach or strategy that works for all. However, it is possible to recognize some patterns that organizations can learn from.

Many have isolated local initiatives before recognizing data and AI as an explicit ingredient in their digital transformation strategy. As mentioned, it is often thanks to those local initiatives that executives learn about the possibilities of these powerful technologies.

Once top management is fully convinced, the next step is creation of an analytics centre of excellence, often in parallel with a data management function (a CDO), to take care of the data and the centre, and create value using analytics and AI. Establishing these two functions is a major step on the data journey. It generates critical mass and transmits a powerful message to the organization, investors and even customers. Businesses that have a well-functioning CDO and analytics centre of excellence for some years will have progressed significantly along their data and AI journey.

A next natural step would be to gradually move analytical capacity out of the centre of excellence, to be closer to the business. In the end, problems need to be solved for the business, not for the centre of excellence. Mature data organizations focus the centre on innovative new applications and technology. Over time, though, its mission shifts from teaching the organization the importance of data and AI to evaluating new technologies and opportunities and bringing the successful new things into the heart of the operation. In short, the focus shifts from change management to innovation. But while the analytics centre of excellence changes its mission, this should not happen to the CDO. Data always needs to be managed company-wide, to maintain 'a single version of the truth.'

CONCLUSION

In summary, a typical and proven path to a successful analytics function looks something like this:

- Activity starts locally, pushed by analytics champions.
- The organization recognizes the importance of analytics and brings fragmented activities together in a centre of excellence.
- A company-wide analytics community is created to connect technical experts with business people.
- The analytics team becomes skilled and experienced by operating for some years as a centre of excellence, nurturing close relationships with the different operating businesses and/or business units.
- Once sufficient analytics maturity is reached, it may make sense to move analytical capacity back to the business, to solve pressing business needs using data and AI.
- The analytics centre of excellence is ultimately refocused on new things and innovation.

Regarding the decisions at the two different levels in multinational corporations, as identified in Figure 13.1, a proven approach is to start the analytics centre of excellence at headquarters, serving the different operating businesses. Once some maturity is achieved, start a centre of excellence in each operating business, and when sufficient maturity and experience exists there, move as much analytical capacity as possible close to the business. This allows maximum scaling of the benefits of data and AI because the analytics capability comes under direct responsibility of the business.

This is the first step in what is called data democratization: moving the benefits of data and AI out of a selected group and bringing it within reach of every single employee. We'll take a closer look at the notion of data democratization in Chapter 17.

WHERE SHOULD YOU RUN THE ANALYTICS, LOCALLY OR GLOBALLY?

THIERRY GRIMA
Group Chief Analytics
Officer, ENGIE [1]

Run it locally or go global? Here we have a perfect example of a simple question, with a not-so-simple answer. First, let's start by defining what the word 'run' means in this context. To me, it is the ability to design, build and operate data and analytics (D&A) solutions.

I've spent 16 of the 22 years of my professional life working for global organizations, all around the world. I've seen many D&A operating models. A secret recipe would need the following ingredients: the company culture, the operating model of the company (centralized, federated or decentralized), the data maturity level (including technology and skills) and the geographical footprint, to name a few.

There is no one-size-fits-all approach. Instead, to be successful, it needs to be flexible enough to adapt to the situation. For instance, as a first step on its data transformation journey, an organization could decide to implement a globally governed D&A practice, since the local D&A capabilities are still low in maturity. The group would therefore support the business entities establishing data methodologies, standards and policies, and also invest in cross-entity use cases to show the value of data. Acculturation can also be part of this initial step, through animating data communities and defining data career paths. On the technical side, the group could also decide to build a global data platform to rationalize costs. The group would then help put the entities into the driving seat.

As a result, local entities would speed up the development of their data foundations, leveraging existing, centrally provided capabilities in different domains, such as skills, data platforms, sharing of best practices/use cases/resources, etc. At some point, the maturity of local entities will be sufficient and the global strategy will need to adapt accordingly.

Besides the need to revisit the D&A strategy regularly, it is advisable to consider other aspects. For instance, developing data use cases using group resources on behalf of an entity is significantly different from helping local entities mature their D&A capabilities so they can develop those same use cases by themselves. Helping through teaching is a much more sustainable model.

Another example comes with the budget: supporting local entities building their D&A foundations doesn't mean that the group needs to pay for everything. After all, something that comes for free often isn't valued enough. Every dollar spent by the group needs to be perceived as an investment contributing to the long-term success of local entities. The group shouldn't hide the real cost of data, but should help entities recognize the cost and unlock the real value.

At the end of the day, data is an asset, and whatever D&A operating model a company goes for, it's important to ensure that it's treated as such within all parts of the organization.

I often see the reporting line of the Chief Data Officer as a way to measure the data maturity of an organization: how far is the CDO away from the CEO? Does he or she belong to IT or a business function, or sit on top of a data office in the middle? Organization of D&A is undoubtedly a significant part of its operating model definition.

14. DATA COLLECTION STRATEGY

So far, we have discussed a lot about data: how to organize it, where to store it, what format to use, etc. But, we haven't discussed where data comes from. That is the subject of this chapter.

Data is not a uniform asset: depending on the sector and organization, there are many different types of data, each with its own peculiarities. It can be structured, unstructured, semi-structured, internal, external, traditional or digital. Therefore, as an organization, it is important to have a data collection strategy that defines what data to collect, and when. Data collection has an associated cost and therefore needs to be part of the budgeting process.

DATA ABUNDANCY

We live in an era of abundant data. Studies show that the amount of data has grown exponentially, from 1-2 exabytes in 2000 to 40,000 exabytes in 2020 (Smith, 2019). And, it will inevitably keep growing in the future. When speaking about data, it's important to distinguish between first-party, second-party and third-party data (Paulina, 2017). In brief, first-party data — also referred to as internal data — is generated by an organization itself, based on its own operations and activity. Second- and third-party data refer to external data sources. An organization accesses second-party data through partnerships, using signed agreements. Third-party data is procured in the market and usually based on a range of external data sources.

Most large organizations start their data and AI journey focusing on first-party data, and this is the main focus of this chapter. First-party data is directly related to the organization's business, and therefore has obvious value for those starting out on their data and AI journey. Some sectors, however, have richer first-party data than others, which might need to rely on second- and third-party data. For instance, telecom, banking and tech giants (the so-called 'GAFA' – Google, Amazon, Facebook and Apple) have rich first-party data, while the insurance sector traditionally is lacking an important part of first-party data. That's because, in that sector, sales and customer relationship data often sit with brokers and agents who manage that part of the value chain. Insurance companies' customer data is often limited to bank account information because that is needed to pay customer claims.

In summary, the fact that there is general data abundancy does not mean that data collection is trivial, easy and free-of-charge. On the contrary, data collection is a complex process that needs to be managed explicitly, as a pivotal element in a data strategy.

FROM TRADITIONAL TO
DIGITAL DATA SOURCES

Companies' traditional data sources include CRM systems, billing data, transactional data, data from physical shops, and data related to customer evaluations, such as the Net Promoter Score (NPS). In itself, collecting and preparing data from those types of sources for analysis and reuse is already a technical and organizational challenge.

As the world and businesses have become increasingly digital, new data sources have entered the picture. These include website data, data from apps, usage data relating to products and services, social media data, call centre content data, location data and others. Moreover, while traditional data was mostly structured, many of the digital data sources are un- or semi-structured, such as call centre content and social media data. Before relevant information can be extracted from such sources, AI technologies, such as NLP, speech recognition and image recognition, are often required.

EXAMPLES OF INTERNAL TELCO DATA SOURCES

Now, let's look at some examples of typical data sources from the telecommunications sector. One of the obvious sources is network data. Telecom providers traditionally collect data on network usage so they can bill customers. Call Detail Records (CDRs) capture customer calls and text messages (SMS). Today, eXtended Detail/Data Records (XDRs) capture data consumption (megabytes uploaded and downloaded). There are CDRs and XDRs for 2G, 3G and 4G, and soon also for 5G. Moreover, there is Quality of Service (QoS) data and location data from antennas carrying the different mobile technologies. As we've seen in other chapters, this network data is very powerful, and also unique in that there aren't many other sectors that can provide the same type of data. The fixed network provides similar types of data related to calls, and internet usage over ADSL and fibre.

Many telecom providers also offer television services, and this generates a new type of data: that relating to TV audiences. This can be used to improve business. Netflix is the king of exploiting this type of data, and is famous for its recommendation algorithm that — based on what you watch, when and how — provides suggestions on what to watch next (Chong, 2020). Netflix has even gone a step further: analysis of audience data helped the network turn its series *House of Cards* into a blockbuster. Using data analytics, Netflix discovered general audience preferences and actually weaved those into the series (Davies, 2019).

Apart from telecom data sources, there are also data sources coming from typical IT systems, such as ERPs, CRMs, HR, etc. They all generate valuable data that can be exploited to create business value.

WHY DATA COLLECTION IS NOT AS EASY AS YOU WOULD THINK

There is a persistent misunderstanding that (large) organizations that generate data have it immediately available for collection, storage and use. In line with this misunderstanding, some even think data dissemination is a simple proposition — data is just there, and sharing it is like disseminating information. Unfortunately, it's not like that at all. Collecting, storing and (re)using quality data is a complex process that requires attention, time, dedication and budget. There are numerous reasons why data collection is harder than it looks at first sight, and worse, some of these may occur simultaneously for the same data source. Let's examine some of these reasons in detail.

YOUR DATA SITS WITH A PROVIDER

Many large organizations have outsourced part of their operation to providers. For instance, your billing system or HR system might be run by an external organization.

You might think this billing and HR data is yours, but physically it lives in the IT systems of the providers. An outsourcing relationship is always covered by a contract. However, you might be surprised how little attention organizations pay to specific clauses related to data access. Traditionally, they focus on the outsourced task being executed correctly, with an adequate SLA. But in the data era, both the execution and *access to* the generated data are important.

The worst situation I've seen is a contract stating that the data is property of the provider and cannot be shared with the client organization. This sounds ridiculous, as the data is clearly entirely about the client organization, but essentially anything a contract stipulates can be enforced as long as the parties sign it. It's therefore important to zero in on such 'abusive' data clauses before signing the contract, when there's still room for negotiation. Once signed, it might be very difficult to change it.

I've also seen situations where there is no clause at all regarding access to data. This is often because both the provider and client think about the service (the task) being performed, and don't think yet about the potential value of the data. When the client organization then asks for data access at some point, different scenarios may play out:

- The provider exports the data to the client organization. Depending on the effort and expense for the provider, this may or may not come with a cost.
- The provider says that it's not feasible to export data, it will have a significant cost and it'll take several months to develop.
- The provider offers access to any data, analytics and insights, but they will provide it for a cost. That is, data access becomes part of the service you contract from the provider. Providers are becoming increasingly aware of the value of data and aim to capture that value themselves, rather than giving it to their customers.

The lesson for organizations is clear: tell your legal department to check all provider contracts (first the new ones and then all existing ones) for data access clauses, and negotiate fair access before signing. While this would seem to be a simple enough procedural process, organizations that lack data maturity have difficulty making it so.

The battle for data: network data

Many years ago, I asked a network provider for some anonymized network data coming from mobile antennas. Up to then, we mostly used CDRs that represent active data (generated when customers call or send an SMS). We wanted to explore what we could do with passive data (generated in the network even if the customer is not doing anything specific with the mobile phone). For example, a mobile phone that moves around will connect to different antennas, and this data is registered somewhere with the provider operating the network. It took me a year and a half, and significant cash outlay, to get a sample of the data. Moreover, I heard many excuses: why it was not possible, that it required significant development, and that it would be costly. Today, the world is more data-mature and this has all become much less complicated.

Many years later, I participated in acquiring a network service from a provider. During the procurement process, which involved a detailed Request for Information (RFI) and Request for Proposal (RFP), there was a workstream focused on accessing and collecting relevant network data. Any provider that wanted to work with us had to explicitly state that this would be possible and give technical details on how access would happen. Much has changed in the five years between these two 'data access' experiences.

The battle for voice data

Almost all large organizations use call centres. Apart from

resolving customer requests, they provide interesting data about complaints, product interest, customer satisfaction, etc. This data is traditionally captured by agents who score the conversation manually in different categories, along with automatic logged data such as day, time, duration and so on. This is a kind of metadata *about* the conversation, which is very helpful for understanding the performance of the call centre itself, as well as providing important insight into company performance. However, there is also a wealth of information in the conversations themselves, when combined with the metadata. And this is where the battle for data access to voice data (audio files) starts.

Data-mature organizations have a high interest in accessing audio files, transcribing them into text and then applying NLP techniques to extract all kinds of relevant information. Sometimes it's even possible to understand the tone of the conversation (angry, emotional, happy, complaining) using audio analytics. Analysis can happen at the aggregated level or, with customer consent, at the individual level. For data-mature organizations it is important to combine this with other types of data. In other words, rather than relegating call centre audio data to a silo, it should be joined up with the other organization data in the data platform.

The reality is that most large organizations either outsource their call centres fully to providers or use a commercial software product that stores and analyses the audio files. Most providers and products can provide audio-to-text transcription and text analytics, but in my experience most providers refuse to give the organization access to raw audio files with the corresponding metadata. They want to provide 'analytics on demand' as part of their business model. This is perfectly understandable from their perspective, but undermines the data (collection) strategy of organizations, as it forces call centre data into a silo.

I fought for many years to get access to raw audio files, without success. The only way to do so was to pay millions of additional euros on top of the existing, costly contract. Apparently, contrary to what happened in the network provider space, the voice provider aspect of all this has managed to stay closed.

The lesson learned is that you should negotiate and agree upon access before contracts are signed, not try to pursue it after.

DATA COLLECTION BY DESIGN

Most large organizations today have an app through which their customers can interact with them and access products and services. You'd be surprised how many of these businesses still only think about the features and functionalities of such an app, and don't consider what data needs to be captured. While some years ago app usage was almost anecdotical compared to more traditional channels, today apps form a basic pillar of any channel strategy. It's therefore important, as part of the data collection strategy, that during the design phase organizations think about what data can be collected — and take explicit decisions about what will be collected — also considering factors such as costs and privacy. While this looks like a simple decision, execution in large organizations is complex. Apps are often specified by a business department and then outsourced to a third party specialized in app development, and data collection is not (or only superficially) considered. There are many stories of apps launched in the market, and when asked about specific usage, the answer is, 'We don't know.' Or, you get the number of downloads as their response. In many cases, it's clear that during the design phase no attention was paid to data collection. Many good lessons on what data to collect and what purpose it serves can be found in the book *Lean Analytics* (Croll and Yoskovitz, 2013).

The important lesson here is that when new channels or products are designed, you should always consider possible data collection. And, as appropriate, the specific app or product should become part of the data collection strategy. Moreover, for good decisions on what data to collect, involvement is needed from data professionals and privacy experts.

COLLECTING DATA REQUIRES DEPLOYMENT ON CUSTOMER PREMISE

Some data collection involves hardware as well as software. For instance, this is the case when collecting TV audience data using set-top boxes (STBs). These devices can be programmed to collect certain types of viewing (audience) data, but until that STB is deployed at a customer premise, it doesn't collect anything, and shipping STBs to customers isn't something organizations want to do all that often. This is an extreme example of data collection being very expensive, but it's important to think deeply about what data should be collected before shipping any STB ... and, of course, to think about the return on investment.

ORGANIZATIONAL SILOS

Even when data collection is only about software, and doesn't involve third-party providers, it can still be a challenge. Many 'traditional' companies still operate in silos: more or less autonomous departments without much coordination and communication. Imagine an organization with a specific department operating the procurement system, where all purchases are processed and stored. Over the years, such a system contains a wealth of data that can be analysed for better understanding of the procurement practice, to detect patterns for cost savings, and even for recommendations on providers for certain categories of purchases. However, if the responsible person is not willing to participate and considers his or her data confidential — not to be shared, apart from high-level reports, with the rest of the organization — it will be hard to collect and store the procurement data in the organization's big data platform. While this is less prevalent as organizations change their mindset as part of their digital transformation, it still happens and needs to be taken into account in the data collection strategy. Otherwise, it might significantly delay execution of the road map.

FROM DATA ACCESS TO DATA STORAGE

It's one thing to have necessary access to data sources, but another to store that data properly, as we've seen in previous chapters. Data sources are usually scattered around the organization, on-premise, in the cloud, with third parties, etc. An effective data collection strategy cannot do without a clear policy on where the accessed data (as described in this chapter) should be stored. It would be wrong to store it locally, close to the data source, as that would lead to data silos. Organizations that are serious about their data journey should have a storage strategy that ensures proper data management (provenance, quality, permissions, etc.) and efficient access for use cases. Any organization can be viewed as a layer of data sources. There are the physical assets that generate data, there is the IT infrastructure, and there are the products and services. All of them generate data that needs to be captured in a coherent and manageable way. In Telefónica, these layers are referred to as the first platform (physical assets), second platform (IT infrastructure), third platform (products and services) and fourth platform (data platform). The data collection strategy states how each platform needs to provide its relevant data to the fourth platform.

PRIVACY OF PERSONAL DATA

It goes without saying that any data collection strategy needs to take into account privacy regulations for data protection, in the event that personal data is collected and stored. In my experience, large organizations have taken a huge leap forward in this respect — thanks in Europe at least to GDPR oversight — and are taking privacy concerns seriously.

OPEN DATA

Finally, there is the question of open data (see Chapter 9), and whether this type of external data should be considered part of an organization's data collection strategy. Open data is published by an organization and can be reused by anyone for free, without limitations (Open Data Institute, 2017). The basic underlying idea is that much more value can be created if data is reused by many, rather than closely guarded by the data holder. In the end, data is a 'non-rivalry good' that isn't depleted and can be reused over and over again.

The use of open data by large organizations is far from being mainstream, but it does happen. For public institutions, openly publishing data is in many countries compulsory, but it's almost non-existent for large corporations. The added value of using open data for organizations is that it is free and can enrich internal data sources. When organizations want to use open data, it should be part of their data collection strategy. While open data may seem too good to be true, we saw in Chapter 9 that there are actually numerous pitfalls associated with using it for business-critical data activities. Let's recap:

- First, since the data is external, there might be doubts about the quality and provenance, and this needs to be understood. Transparency is important here.
- Second, most data becomes obsolete after some time and needs to be updated or refreshed. Open data is not always reliable regarding the stated frequency of updates.
- Third, there's the liability problem. Open data is usually provided for free (by public institutions) because this is compulsory. But the obligation is about the publishing, not about quality or updates. So, if an organization uses open data somewhere in its data value chain, and the open data part fails (out of date, not available, etc.), you have a problem. If an organization uses open data in paid services to customers, who is responsible (legally liable) for the service not being delivered? Is it the organization or the provider of open data? In practice, it is not the open data publisher who's liable, so organizations need to be aware of that.

WHAT SHOULD A DATA COLLECTION STRATEGY COVER?

It should now be clear why a coherent data strategy is necessary for organizations that want to create consistent, sustainable value from data. Data collection cannot be taken for granted, and not explicitly considering this in the data strategy will invariably lead to delays and frustrations when wanting to solve business problems with data and AI.

When designing a data collection strategy, organizations should consider the following:

- **What data to collect, and when.** As we have seen in this chapter, data should be collected based on use cases (business needs determine what data is needed) and data collection should be considered each time new products and services that will generate data are designed. Priorities and available resources will help shape the road map.
- **Where and how to store the data.** This relates to the earlier discussion around cloud versus on-premise (Chapter 11) and local or global storage, or a unified data model (Chapter 12). Is the data stored centrally, or locally in the geographies? Is it stored in the cloud or on-premise? And, is the data stored as is, or defined by the local business? Alternatively, is it stored in a unified data model? Those decisions are important, as they have an impact on timing and budget.
- **Estimation of costs and budget assignment.** As we have learned in this chapter, data collection is not a trivial process, contrary to popular belief. Therefore, without assigning budget for this activity, it's not likely to happen, and definitely not as planned.
- **Efforts to break data silos.** While organizations may not want to write this explicitly in a strategy document, the people factor is also important to consider. Still, some large, traditional organizations consist of a set of uncoordinated, scarcely communicating silos. Breaking these silos, by requiring that their data be stored in a company-wide data platform, may meet with initial resistance. While this resistance makes no sense from an organizational point of view, it does from a human perspective. In the end, data is power, and people don't like to lose power. Ignoring this factor might again lead to delays and frustration.

15. WORKING WITH EXTERNAL PROVIDERS AND PARTNERS

Many organizations, at some point during their data and AI journey, decide to work with third parties. This chapter is about why organizations do that, the different modes of collaboration, as well as lessons learned about what works and potential pitfalls.

WHY ORGANIZATIONS WORK WITH THIRD PARTIES FOR DATA, ANALYTICS AND AI

There are many reasons why organizations hire others to support them with their data and AI journey. Here are a few of them:

LACK OF KNOWLEDGE AND EXPERIENCE

A typical motivation for organizations that have just decided to start the journey is that they simply don't know how and where to start. There are many data and analytics providers that are able to do whatever is needed to help them get rolling. An example would be implementing the first use case, which would include data collection, data quality assessment and the analytics for solving the particular problem.

Another example would be to set up (and operate) a big data platform, or perform a use case discovery exercise to identify what the most attractive use cases are for the particular organization.

CREATE MORE 'DATA' BANDWIDTH

Another common reason to work with third parties is to increase the bandwidth of the internal data teams. This often happens when organizations have already made progress on their data journey and achieved some successes. Good results motivate organizations to do more, but if the team has no capacity to grow, outsourcing activities, such as specific use cases, makes sense. A related financial reason may be that the organization wants to do more and there is budget available. However, it is not uncommon that, while there is budget for operational expenditure, the data and AI departments are not allowed to take on additional headcount. In this case, outsourcing makes sense, because the activity grows but the headcount doesn't increase.

CREATE MORE SUPPORTING IT BANDWIDTH

As we have seen in Chapter 2, there's a close relationship between data and IT. A big data platform is an IT system, after all, and in many organizations its operation, maintenance and evolution are the responsibility of the IT team. There are, however, many other areas in the organization that also require support from IT. Therefore, the data team's progress may depend on a scheduled action by the IT team, based on global priorities, that may not come until several weeks or even months down the road. If this blocks an important data project, the data department might decide to contract the task to an external provider, just to be able to move forward. The best way to do this is in close coordination with the IT team, in such a way that, when the IT slot for the data team has arrived, the IT team knows exactly what has been done by the external provider and can act efficiently.

EXTERNAL ASSESSMENT OF DATA-RELATED ACTIVITIES

Companies that have progressed for a few years on their data and AI journey, and have several technologies, processes and organizational processes in place, might wonder whether they're still on the right track. Their decisions have gotten them where they are, which is usually a much better place than where they started. Yet, they want to be sure that before investing even more in their current way of working, they're taking the correct decisions moving forward. And so, it would be wise to take a step back and ask an external specialist to assess and evaluate the current data (and analytics and AI) situation. Such assessments usually consist of interviews and studying relevant documents (IT, processes, HR policy, organizational structure, security, privacy, etc.) to document the state of affairs. After conversations with executives, experts and data leaders in the organization, a vision of where it wants to be in the future is drawn up. Finally, the specialist company collaborates with the organization to create a road map that leads from here to there, including planning, responsibilities and a budget estimate.

INNOVATION AND NEW, COOL THINGS

Another reason organizations want to work with external partners is for innovation. Outside expertise can help them learn about the newest things in data and AI, and understand whether they'd address business problems or opportunities the organization is facing. This usually involves some kind of collaboration with start-ups or universities. When organizations start to look for innovative solutions beyond what's available in the market, this normally means they already have significant experience with data, analytics and AI. So, they've already made real progress on their data and AI journey.

DATA DEMOCRATIZATION

Organizations that have reached a certain level of data maturity (see Chapter 4), and have effectively functioning data teams in place to create value, might want to start looking at how to democratize this new capability beyond the data professionals. If significant value is created by the data teams, imagine how much more can be created if a larger part of the organization would be involved. Data democratization is a complex process that involves new technology, new processes and HR participation for training and workshops. Since democratization is a key component of becoming a data-driven company, we'll look at that in depth in the pages ahead (Chapter 17).

MODES OF COLLABORATION WITH THIRD PARTIES

There are several ways of collaborating with third parties; they vary depending on the ultimate objective. Let's examine a few of them.

- For short-term or one-off collaborations, a suitable option is to externalize the activity to a third party through a project-based or a time- and material-based contract. This is a suitable collaboration mode if the objective is to 'get it done' and there's no compelling need to learn from the externalized activity, apart from a basic knowledge transfer as part of the contract.

- For long-term collaborations, a partnership is a more suitable option. A partnership is based on a trusted relationship and a fair interchange of value. Good partnerships are win-win propositions, where the third party has confidence in recurrent revenues without tough negotiations for each activity. And, the contracting party can rely on honest, transparent reporting and quality work without fear of being locked in to a bad business relationship. Moreover, a true partnership allows for open knowledge transfer in both directions.

- Another mode of collaboration aims to internalize an activity within the organization. It may be a new data and AI activity the company has no experience with but wants to initiate. It hires a third party to implement this activity in the organization, and it makes sure that, once implemented, the organization is able to operate, maintain and evolve the activity by itself. A variant of this type of collaboration is the BOT (Build, Operate and Transfer) model. Such a collaboration starts with outsourcing the activity and building a system that's then operated by the third party. Once the system is up and running, initial problems have been solved and things are performing well, the operation and knowledge are transferred to the organization to run, maintain and evolve independently.

- A final way of collaborating is through acquisition or investment, or a combination of these. When organizations have the data and analytics basics in place and are generating value in a consistent and systematic way, they might want to scale up significantly in a short period of time. Growing organically takes time, as people need to be hired, onboarded and trained. In such situations, acquisition of a niche company might make sense. Imagine, for instance, a large company that's built up a significant data capability both at headquarters and in its operating businesses. If it suddenly wants to double its capacity and accelerate progress on the data journey, it might acquire a consultancy to double its data professionals headcount overnight. This is what Telefónica did in 2015 when it acquired the big data boutique consultant Synergic Partners.[1] A less aggressive way to rapidly extend capabilities is to invest in a data company, assign activities of the organization to it, and depending on the result, increase or reduce this activity ... or even acquire the company entirely.

Whatever the mode of collaboration, working with third parties has the additional advantage of bringing in external market expertise, which the organization wouldn't otherwise have access to.

CONCRETE EXPERIENCES AND POTENTIAL PITFALLS

In this section, I will describe some real collaboration experiences, in specific situations, without naming the organizations involved. Making organizations aware of such situations can help them take explicit decisions on how to deal with them.

In one project, I worked with an external consultancy to help scale up a successful, but complex, use case to various operating businesses. We had done some operating businesses ourselves and wanted to accelerate the implementation in the group. Our objective was to obtain more bandwidth, but in the longer term maintain and evolve the resulting system ourselves. This required a fully transparent solution. The provider had problems with this because it saw the knowledge as valuable intellectual property, gained from working with other companies, and wasn't willing to provide full transparency. The fear was that we would sell the solution ourselves and compete directly with the provider.

In another project, we worked with a different consultant to perform a typical analytics/AI use case for churn prediction. We had budget, but were not allowed to increase headcount. In this case, we got full collaboration and transparency on all the code generated, with a complete knowledge transfer that allowed us to run the resulting system ourselves.

In yet another project, we worked with a large consultancy on a video analytics project. This consultant subcontracted the analytics work to yet another company, which was not as expert in the matter as we'd expected. Both factors led to a complex interaction, and in the end we had to pull the plug on the project before it was finished.

Another project saw us acquire a license from a major big data platform provider, and contract maintenance through an expensive SLA. However, since the provider was in a different time zone, the office hours didn't overlap, and there were significant perceived lags in the service, leading to disruptively long delays.

A final experience was a project where we hired a consultant to help us discover use cases and prioritize them according to financial impact to the business. The consultant had significant experience in the relevant sector and was able to deliver benefit by realistically estimating the financial impact.

CONCLUSION

In this chapter we have seen why an organization would want to work with third parties for data-related activities. We've also seen different types of collaboration, along with their advantages and disadvantages. An organization's data maturity is an important factor in deciding on the best form of collaboration.

Organizations that are at an early stage of the data journey are likely to count on third parties to harness external expertise and to start specific initiatives. Organizations that have already progressed along their journey often need external help to scale up and accelerate activities, after which the activities are internalized in the organization's data teams. More data-mature organizations look for innovations in data and consider investing in — or even acquiring — data, analytics or AI companies to speed up their journey.

Whenever organizations work with third parties, they should always be careful to avoid lock-ins, where it becomes hard to change to another vendor because most (if not all) knowledge is with the third party and not with the organization. In addition, lock-ins may lead to higher prices because the provider knows that switching to another provider would be even more expensive for the organization.

LESSONS FOR OUTSOURCING
BIG DATA AND AI

**BASSEY
HARRISON
UMOH**
Senior Manager,
Customer Analytics
and Insights, MTN
Nigeria

With the proliferation in big data, machine learning and advanced analytics, many organizations are afraid of missing out on the action. And so, a growing number have jumped in, pursuing initiatives to deliver the perceived benefits of becoming a data-driven company.

Yet, a lot of them have not fully understood how to go about executing these projects. More importantly, they don't know how and where to start. Furthermore, they haven't really considered two of the key reasons most of these projects fail: data access and data quality. As improbable as it seems, there are organizations that have embarked on a data transformation journey but haven't really considered data a key strategic asset.

The organization MUST perform a maturity assessment before commencing a data or digital transformation journey, to evaluate where it stands, identify gaps and plot out the steps to move it toward the desired end state.

In my experience, organizations often miss this crucial step, and focus mainly on technology delivery. Some go ahead and issue RFPs to vendors who don't fully understand the business and how it can (and should) utilize data as a key strategic resource. The organization must be deliberate about its data transformation journey, and it must be sponsored by the highest level of management.

Organizations can select different vendors to handle either the big data or analytics projects, or they can opt for the same vendor. The decision to do this is entirely up to them.

Depending on the outcome of the maturity assessment

— which must be an outside-in process — the organization can then decide to outsource some or all of the elements of the big data and analytics project, to one or more vendors. Or, it can decide to implement the project itself, if it has in fact developed or acquired the expertise to do so in-house.

If there's a decision to outsource to one vendor, the supplier must be able to demonstrate that it has successfully executed projects at the necessary scale, and can do so for the hiring organization.

Vendors must demonstrate experience along the following dimensions in order to deliver a robust data driven strategy. (My telecom services company has adapted these requirements from Telefónica's vetting criteria.)

- **Case Discovery.** This process helps prioritize use cases that are feasible, have high business impact, and fully utilize the organization's data resources to maximize the value of big data and analytics.
- **Governance.** Employ data governance principles, procedures and policies that are best suited to the organization and optimize the value of data.
- **Organizational Development.** This encompasses operational and human dimensions and is best executed by conducting a maturity assessment.
- **Big data Architecture.** This is defined by the technology road map for the execution of the big data/analytics ecosystem required for the implementation of use cases. Unfortunately, most organizations put too much focus on this, to their detriment.
- **Strategy Adoption & Deployment Road map.** This includes a comprehensive list of tasks, actions and deliverables that must be executed to enable the organization to evolve across the dimensions stated above.

In conclusion, organizations that choose to outsource must ensure that the vendor can demonstrate how its execution will transform the organization across the areas mentioned above, in relation to their current status. From experience, I've learned that the ideal vendor will effectively execute across all these dimensions. More importantly, the vendor must engage with the business to fully understand how it intends to use data as a key strategic resource, to become truly data-driven.

The vendor must engage with all the business units, and the execution must be business-led, not IT-led. It is futile for the vendor to work offsite, especially when it's situated in close proximity to the organization. Furthermore, within a multi-country organization, the central or group office typically drives the process. If so, the organization must ensure that implementation is handled on a case-by-case basis. It is best to pilot with a few operating countries, and ensure that the vendor is 100% in-country throughout the planning and execution phases. The operating businesses within the group that will serve as the pilot should be involved during the vendor selection stage, and must have executive sponsorship.

The vendor and the business must see themselves as partners in this journey, and a tight relationship must exist among all the teams involved in the project.

PART IV

PEOPLE

The fourth part of this book is about people. At the time of writing, all strategic decisions about data and AI (and beyond) are still taken by real, live people. That might change at some point in the future, (Benjamins and Salazar, 2020), but today it is still people that decide.

The human resources of a corporation — its employees — play an important role in the speed of adoption of AI and big data. Having the right organizational culture is essential. An inadequate culture will put the brakes on the data transformation, and bring everything to a screeching halt.

16. WINNING OVER SCEPTICS

Even if the strategy of an organization is well defined and clearly communicated, there are always those who will be sceptical, and will actively resist change. In large organizations, this is all too common — it almost always happens and needs to be dealt with. Data is not different in this respect. While it is best practice to not start the change with sceptics, but rather with 'champions' or early adopters, in some cases one needs to work with sceptics. This is especially true when they are the owner of important data or responsible for a business area that's been chosen to run a big data or AI use case (see Chapter 6).

WHAT MOTIVATES SCEPTICS?

The following scenario is not uncommon. You have performed your opportunity matrix analysis to select the best use cases, balancing business impact with feasibility. But then, when you start talking to the business owner who would be impacted by the use case, he or she tells you something like, "I've done this for many years and I don't need anything else to do my job." Or, "I already know what my restrictions are (business goals, regulation, etc.), so there's nothing to add." You may hear, "I don't need AI or

big data until you can show me how it has worked successfully, and what the results were, elsewhere for a business
like mine." And there you go. You started the meeting very
enthusiastically, but left frustrated, wondering why there
was this resistance.

There can be many reasons for such reactions. A few of
them include:

- General resistance to change. Many people are working in their comfort zone and will resist anything that
moves them out of that familiar space.
- Fear of not doing the job properly. Analytical use cases
are almost always about improving business or reducing costs. A business owner might feel that if a data/
analytics department demonstrates that such improvement is possible, he or she might be criticized for not
having proposed the same initiative earlier.
- Concern over being seen as not innovative. Today, many
organizations place a lot of importance on innovation
and expect leaders to explore and apply innovations as
part of BAU.
- Collaborating in a data, analytics or AI initiative requires
sharing data across the business area, and this automatically implies becoming transparent. Before, the business
owner controlled the data, decided how to interpret it
and presented the conclusions. Now, others would be
able to do the same. This leads to the impression of having less control (and power) and invariably exposes the
business owner to more criticism than before.

For these reasons, and more, it's not strange to have such a
frustrating first meeting. But, what are the lessons learned
to win over those who are resistant to new data and analytics initiatives?

STRATEGIES TO WORK
SUCCESSFULLY WITH SCEPTICS

The natural reaction when a head of some part of the business refuses to cooperate on a data or AI initiative is to escalate, and then use formal authority to compel participation. Depending on the seniority of the business owner, formal authority means that two senior executives have a conversation, or it means a direct order to get on board. Whatever the approach, a formal authority might force the business owner to accept, but not in an optimal way. He or she may say yes to all, but actually act in a 'no' manner, or perhaps come up with all kinds of excuses and artificial hurdles (privacy, security and confidentiality concerns are popular ones) that block progress. Or, the person may simply assign insufficient resources, which leads to delays and lack of traction.

While there is no recipe that always works to convince sceptical people, there are some lessons learned that have worked in the past:

- Find a champion in the business area who is interested in exploring new ways of doing things, and who loves innovation.
- Keep the initial collaboration below the radar.
- Start working together, build trust, understand the problem and find the sweet spot where data or AI can really improve the business head's situation.
- Work on a prototype, discuss the results with the champion, and make sure he or she fully understands the positive business impact.
- Have the champion socialize the prototype results across the business area.
- Enlist the champion to show the work and results to the business owner, emphasizing that control and ownership of the project reside fully with the business area.

If the business owner understands the essence of the work, and views it as an activity of his or her area, it won't be seen as a threat. Instead, it'll present itself as an opportunity to show innovation and improvement coming from the area itself. Once you've gotten to that point, the business owner will likely function as a spokesperson for data and AI, evangelizing to the rest of the organization.

A key aspect of this approach is that ownership and leadership of the project, and the credit for the results, are with the business area from the start. Data, analytics and AI departments often claim ownership and credit for results, downplaying the effort the business area put into getting them. In practice, that has an adverse effect. However, if successfully positioned within the business area, credit and recognition will be given to the data and analytics/AI teams as well. If not publicly, at least benefit will flow to the analytics and AI operation in the form of budget for the next year.

A mistake I made early on was to complete a successful analytics initiative with a business unit, and then publicize the project and results in company forums and executive meetings without notifying or involving the business unit. Obviously, this wasn't appreciated by that part of the business, and it never happened again.

CONCLUSION

When starting new data, analytics or AI initiatives, it always pays to begin with business owners who are eager to collaborate — those true champions of change. However, if for some reason this isn't possible, and you have to work with sceptical business owners, try to make the business area the recognized owner of the project, so it's viewed as coming from inside rather than outside. And, give full credit to the business area. Over time, almost all sceptical business owners turn around and even become evangelists for AI and big data. Be patient; it may take many months or even a year or more. (If not, they're likely to retire soon anyway!)

There's one other important aspect to take into account when starting data/analytics initiatives in large organizations that apply to all business areas. Don't forget to involve any relevant area or department. If they're not involved (when they should be) they might work as detractors rather than as facilitators. In large companies, there are generally central HQ areas with corresponding local areas in the operating businesses. For example, in data/AI/analytics, there is usually a department at headquarters and also one in each operating business. For a particular use case — let's say, to improve marketing campaigns — there is the global marketing area, under the CMO, and the local marketing area. And, for many data initiatives, there's also an important IT role, which exists at both the global level and the local level. The lesson is that any initiative should involve both the relevant global and local areas to become fully successful. If not, apart from hurting feelings, somewhere along the value chain the initiative may grind to a halt or at least face damaging delays.

For instance, a marketing analytics project that does not involve the local marketing area from the beginning will run into problems when a pilot needs to be performed. That simply can't be done without the local marketing team. The local team isn't necessarily needed for designing the technology and the marketing approach, because the global marketing team has all the required knowledge and experience.

Of course, the downside is that at the start of any initiative, too many areas and people are involved in the meetings. The best way to avoid this is to host a kickoff meeting with all potentially involved areas, and then activate individual areas when they're needed. This way, at least they're aware of the project and bought into it to some extent. (If not, you can use the lessons learned that we've explored in this chapter.)

17. **DATA DEMOCRATIZATION**

When organizations have their basic data functions in place — taking care of data access and quality, analytics and machine learning, and delivering real value to the business — this means that they've reach a certain degree of data maturity. That's the time to take the next step and scale up value creation beyond a small, selected group of data professionals.

For growing value creation with data after the initial phases, there are two approaches, which are not necessarily mutually exclusive:

- Grow the data and analytics departments with more resources so they can cover more projects.
- Democratize the data and analytics capabilities so that more people in the organization can deliver (and derive) value.

As we will see in this chapter, there is a tipping point when data democratization becomes more effective than a big data and AI initiative would be if grown centrally.

GROWING DATA TEAMS TO
COVER MORE DEMAND FOR
INSIGHTS AND ANALYTICS

The step organizations normally take when the data basics are in place is to grow their data teams, to be able to cover more ground. At this stage, organizations have understood, especially at the top, that data generates financial value, and that there's a clear return on investment. Therefore, they're ready for more investments to grow the economic value of data.

Growing the data organization is similar to expanding upon the centre of excellence approach (Chapter 13). Once there is sufficient business traction, the risk of this team of experts performing analytics for the sake of analytics — without an identified business need — is almost non-existent. However, it's still important to establish close relationships with the different business areas. For example, it pays to establish a business partner sort of model, where specific people have responsibility for bridging the gap between key business areas and the analytics capabilities. Another key element of this approach (growing a centre of excellence) is to establish a cross-organization data or analytics board. This group periodically decides how to assign the limited central data and analytics resources to business areas. To track and manage the increasing demands on the data and analytics team, a demand-management system becomes necessary to address the priorities in a systematic and consistent manner.

But, in increasing use of data and analytics to create value, there's a limit on how much a central team can grow to deal with increasing demand and remain efficient. Prioritization through the data or analytics board becomes harder over time, as it's impossible to satisfy all business needs, and business areas will inevitably become impatient.

This is the moment when organizations need to make the next step. They need to democratize the data capability, putting it into the hands of more and more employees, so they become data self-sufficient.

DATA DEMOCRATIZATION

The process of data democratization means that progressively more employees are empowered with the capability to create value from data through the notion of self-service. If you think of an organization as consisting of different layers with data needs, more layers can gradually become involved, leveraging the layers to empower the next layer. This is the way to scale data through an organization without the need for large investments. If Layer 0 is the centre of excellence, Layer 1 could be the next 250 employees who most need data (and are able to learn the technical requisites). Once those 250 people are up to speed, they could involve the next layer of 250 employees — always under supervision of the centre of excellence, with the support of HR — until the whole organization becomes data- and analytics-empowered.

While all types of analytics in the past were performed by a team of engineers (data professionals, such as data scientists, data engineers and statisticians), today several tools exist that overlay complex engineering tasks with easy-to-use interfaces. This is a trend that will continue; more and more engineering tasks will become doable by tech-savvy non-engineers. Of course, it's impossible to cover the full data and analytics value chain through self-service, but it is possible to democratize parts by providing tools that are friendly to a wider swathe of users with business or commercial responsibility.

SELF-SERVICE DATA
AND ANALYTICS TOOLS

There are currently three types of self-service tools available in the market: for descriptive analytics, predictive analytics and prescriptive analytics. Figure 17.1 provides an overview of these three types of analytics (McNellis, 2019), enabled by increasing data maturity. All can be used by tech-savvy business users, but training is needed before they can actually be used to explore or create real value.

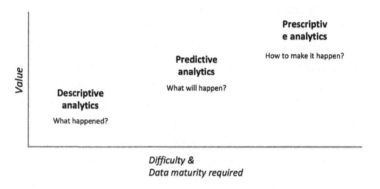

Figure 17.1 Three types of analytics – descriptive, predictive and prescriptive – enabled by increasing data maturity (McNellis, 2019)

TOOLS FOR DESCRIPTIVE ANALYTICS

Descriptive analytics looks backwards, to what has happened, and contributes to understanding how the business (or certain activity) is evolving over time. Examples include the best performing sales locations in the last month, profitability of regions over the past 12 months, number of web visits and their geographical origin in the previous seven days, etc. Descriptive analytics is the first step organizations need to take when gaining access to data. This basic analytics activity provides relevant insights on how the business is developing, viewed from many different perspectives. Typically, descriptive analytics provides visual representations of data in the form of dashboards.

Today, there are many visual tools available on the market that allow non-engineers to create any visualization the data permits, through a simple drag and drop user interface. Typical examples include Tableau, Qlik, Spotfire, Power BI, MicroStrategy and Data Studio. These tools allow you to connect to data in a database or a spreadsheet — either locally, on the internet or in the cloud — and provide an easy-to-use graphical interface to build dashboards. There are many subtle differences between the tools, but their mission is the same. There are also more advanced tools, such as ThoughtSpot, which is able to crawl through the data by itself and suggest possible ways to explore, analyse and visualize it. This particular tool even has a voice interface. The tools also differ in that varying degrees of programming skills are needed, especially for the more advanced features, but it's generally a matter of getting used to the tool and sorting through personal preferences. In large organizations, it's often the IT department that selects the corporate tools that employees can use in their professional environment.

With these tools, dashboards that were typically developed by skilled engineers and programmers can now be created by non-engineers, or even tech-savvy business people. They represent a viable and effective way to democratize data beyond the data department. Such tools allow business people to explore data by themselves without having to ask the data or IT experts to create a report or update a dashboard.

TOOLS FOR PREDICTIVE ANALYTICS

While tools for self-service descriptive analytics are increasingly becoming a commodity, self-service tools for predictive analytics have started to appear and are being used by early adopters. Such tools take as input quality data and, through a graphical user interface, allow business users to run different types of machine-learning algorithms. These include both supervised and unsupervised machine learning, with structured data (Excel spreadsheets, databases) and unstructured data (text, such as reviews, or images). Moreover, most of these tools run in the cloud and on-premise if requested. Examples include BigML[1] and DataRobot. The basic dynamic is that business users upload data, check some basic quality aspects and then select a machine-learning algorithm to run on that data set. For example, this could be a prediction or classification task in instances of supervised learning, or a topic model of reviews in unsupervised learning situations. Figure 17.2, Figure 17.3 and Figure 17.4 illustrate a typical process using BigML: checking basic data quality aspects, creating the predictive model and testing its performance. All these tasks can be performed quite simply by a business person, without any support from a technical engineer.

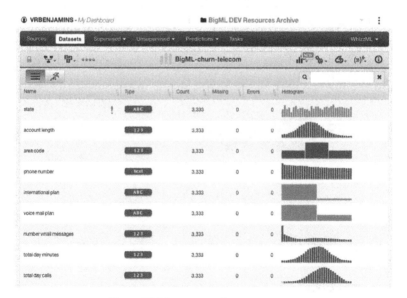

Figure 17.2 Basic data quality check in BigML

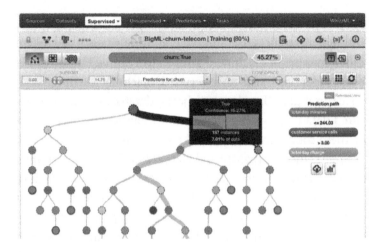

Figure 17.3 A decision tree generated automatically by BigML for churn prediction. The main reasons customers leave a brand are the total number of daily minutes called, and the number of calls to, the customer call centre.

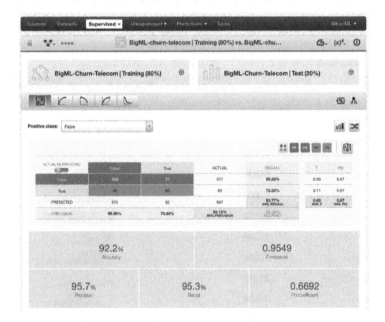

Figure 17.4 The result of evaluating the performance of the prediction model for churn using a confusion matrix

At present, there really aren't any business-friendly tools for performing prescriptive analytics, which remains in the realm of data scientists.

TRAINING WORKSHOPS

Of course, training is necessary for business people to learn how to work with these self-service tools. Almost all tool providers offer education and training, both in-person and online, involving extensive video tutorials and webinars. At the same time, apart from learning to use specific tools, it's also wise for organizations to organize workshops for employees, to provide a better understanding of the value of data for business. In the end, tools are important, but the success or failure of becoming more data driven is in large part determined by the culture and data maturity of an organization. A good book to read on this, which we cited earlier, is *Lean Analytics* (Croll and Yoskovitz, 2013).

TOOLS FOR DATA MANAGEMENT

While more tools are becoming available for descriptive and predictive analytics, they all assume that data is available and that it has sufficient quality. However, if data quality isn't verified, you don't know whether some data-driven phenomenon is due to a business event or an error in the data. Unfortunately, there aren't many tools that enable business people to gain access to, check and produce quality data. While some tools represent a step forward in the process of democratizing data access and quality, they're primarily used by data engineers. Examples of these include Trifacta, DataIQ and Talend.

And so, while with sufficient data maturity you can democratize descriptive and predictive analytics across the organization using the tools we've discussed, it wouldn't be wise to democratize data as the 'single source of the truth' across the organization, with each department or business person accessing, curating and maintaining their own data.

CONCLUSION

One of the consequences of self-service is that the data and analytics department is relieved of some of the more repetitive tasks. This is a win-win. Data professionals (engineers, scientists) are motivated by challenging, hard problems, not by simple tasks. Business people do value the ability to create basic insights and data exploration on their own, without the need to log a formal request in a demand management system. The organization wins by increased speed to decisions and agility. At the same time, some who are part of the analytics and AI departments may move closer to the business, becoming part of business units, where they can share their analytics and AI knowledge and accelerate data democratization across the organization.

Over time, this change also refocuses the role of the analytics and AI departments toward more innovative activities. They become the gateway for promising new technologies, test them for business impact, and discard or promote them based on prototypes and pilots.

There are two major lessons learned here:
- Start the data journey by grouping dispersed people with data activities into a central group of data professionals, to create critical mass in relevant knowledge and experience. But, once a certain degree of data maturity is reached, move some champions back to the business units to drive the democratization process.
- Use self-service tools to empower tech-savvy business-people with analytics capabilities.

- The data itself needs to remain centralized and carefully managed as an asset. All analytics and AI need to run on top of data that is quality-certified.

BUSINESS DRIVEN AI! A PARADIGM SHIFT AWAY FROM DATA SCIENCE

JAN W VELDSINK
MSc Knowledge
Engineering (AI)
Lead AI and Cognitive
Technologies
Rabobank Compliance

When we started AI and machine learning at the bank in 2008, working at finding fraud, AI was strictly an IT domain thing, where we as specialists stepped into the business space to do the modelling. In subsequent years, we moved toward a more democratic view of this activity.

A few years ago, I stated that every initiative should involve AI and data, and would have to be strictly non-coding. A lot of IT staff were horrified with the idea that non-IT employees could actually create and run algorithms like AI and machine learning.

Now, what was a dream in 2010 has become reality. We are able to assist business tasks with these capabilities and support the business with self-service AI/ML. To get there, the business needed to develop in-depth knowledge of AI/ML. And this is far better than what I observed in the past: AI/ML without any domain knowledge (general data science practice).

In our bank, we're en route to a more data-driven business, and new environments like BigML[2] are necessary to support the business data-driven tasks. IT staff are responsible for setting up the data and platform for the business to perform its AI tasks.

For example, we introduced data-driven audits, where we trained the auditors to start using ML on the data they received. Previously, they put the data into a spreadsheet and tried to find the interesting questions to ask in the audit. That process took them more than two weeks. Imagine 30 columns with over 5,000 records. If you were lucky, you'd perhaps be able to manually find the anomalies. Placing the same data in the (Big)ML platform and

performing an anomaly detection task delivers the crucial questions to ask in less than half an hour, and with a far more interesting outcome.

AI/ML is all about asking the right questions so we can resolve
our challenges with the technology. And, the only source of the
right question is the business that has the urge to optimize and
have its decisions supported. The IT department will not be able
to phrase the right question (other than for optimizing their own
business), address the right data and appreciate the outcome of an
AI project.

To summarize, here are the lessons learned:

- Start with the question.
- AI/ML is a business task.
- Organize AI/ML expertise and knowledge in your domain.
- Split IT and business responsibilities.
- Data and business understanding is key.
- Use platforms for AI/ML, like BigML.
- Start with the application in mind.
- Skip data science and go for 'decision engineering' — the art
  of augmenting data science with theory from social science,
  decision theory and managerial science.

Application areas, in my banking compliance experience, have
included things like fraud, anti-money-laundering (AML), 'know your
customer' (KYC), data quality, ledger routing, phishing mail classification, credit default prediction, automated risk detection and more.

18. HOW TO CREATE MOMENTUM WITH DATA

Let's take a look at the challenges typically encountered in a new department focused on creating value from data through analytics and AI. The initial steps are likely dedicated to data access, preparation and understanding. For small experiments, those steps may take weeks, but when working on large use cases involving a significant amount of periodically updated data, it may take months or even longer. This has been highlighted elsewhere in this book (e.g. Chapter 14 on data collection).

When the first results become available — such as a well-performing analytical or machine-learning model — the data teams get excited, and want to improve the model just a little bit, and then a bit more, before communicating the results to management.

As a result, the data teams and their direct managers are well aware of what's going on, and might be satisfied with the results, but the rest of the organization is mostly unaware of it. Data scientists and engineers are usually more focused on the work done than on communicating their results. Moreover, results can always be improved, and the teams often prefer to improve rather than communicate, just to be sure that what they'll communicate is correct and cannot be questioned. This is good, and they should continue to strive for high quality. There is, however, also a downside to this approach: not putting effort into effective communication implies that for the rest of the organization the data teams hardly exist.

THE PROBLEM

Senior executives tend to give important strategic decisions a certain amount of time to show results. That period is typically 18-24 months (see Chapter 8). Data teams, and technical teams in general, spend this time working on the problem, and leave it to their direct managers and other levels in the hierarchy to inform the organization. While this may work, there's a risk that the direct managers are not communicating well. This is probably not the rule, but it happens often enough. One consequence might therefore be that both senior executives and the organization at large are only vaguely aware of the progress being made by the data teams. In principle, this is not a problem, because of 'patience' leeway up front.

When the 18-month honeymoon period is almost over, the direct managers usually receive a request from senior executives to show them the results, and the data teams and their direct managers work hard to produce a presentation and demo. This often culminates in a slot of 20 minutes (or perhaps an hour, if lucky) that is the moment of fame or failure. In case of failure, there is usually another six months to improve.

In parallel, if in the beginning it was publicly stated that new data teams were created with significant investments, while other departments might have suffered cost reductions, there might exist some unrest in the organization as blame is directed at the data teams for taking too much of 'their' budget. This is more likely to happen if no clear results have been communicated. All of this has a negative impact on the climate within the company. This dynamic is more common than you might think, and likely to repeat itself in many different new areas.

CREATING A POSITIVE SPIN – MOMENTUM

There is another approach where your fate doesn't depend on a 20-minute presentation to the board. The basic principle is to make it hard for senior executives and the rest of the organization not to hear about your activities, without having any specific meeting to present to them. The approach consists of proactively communicating positive and impactful activities and results. Let's see how that can be done.

To start, establish good relations with the Communications department, for both internal and external communication purposes. Data and AI are hot topics nowadays, with interest inside and outside the organization – for instance, among the press. Remember that if you don't communicate what you do, it effectively doesn't exist beyond your own area.

Select the right portfolio of activities and use cases to publicize. In Chapter 6 we discussed how to select use cases based on an opportunity matrix of business impact and feasibility. We saw that at the beginning of the data journey it's important to sometimes prioritize feasibility over business impact. This is tied to the organization's initial 'patience period' of roughly 18 months. When we want to create enthusiasm for data and AI, an additional criterion to consider is how 'communicable' the use case is. And here we have to consider its power for internal communication, but also for external publicity (general business press, sector-specific trades, blogs, industry panels and speaking engagements, etc.).

The reason is both simple and very human. When evaluating the importance of something, the more sources we have that mention or discuss the activity in a positive way, the more importance we tend to give to them. It's all about recognition: have the wider organization and even the external world recognize the value of your data activity, and the likelihood will increase that senior managers and the wider organization recognize it as well. Compare these two scenarios:

1. Only the data teams know the results, and their managers get 20 minutes or so to convince the board of their initiatives' relevance, value and longer-term viability.
2. Most of the organization knows about the results, which have appeared in the press and in blogs, and now the managers get 20 minutes to present to the well-primed board.

See the difference? This is a lesson I learned first hand. Scenario 1 is the traditional way of doing things, but scenario 2 is so much easier — and so much more fun — even though it involves more work. You can't imagine the impact on team motivation if you follow scenario 2.

HOW TO SELECT A 'COMMUNICABLE' USE CASE

One thing to take into account when communicating a use case is that it should not reveal any confidential information, or put privacy at risk, since the impact would be the opposite of the goal. A good candidate use case for communicating widely might be one related to using data to help achieve the UN's sustainable development goals (United Nations, 2015). Showing that the organization is committed to advancing these admirable objectives creates a purpose, and has a positive impact on motivation and reputation. Another good option might be to partner with humanitarian organizations, such as UNICEF or UN Global Pulse, who have dedicated data teams to contribute to sustainable development. While there is a risk that such projects do not directly contribute to short-term business goals, they establish the data teams as a recognized, highly professional resource (solving those problems is hard) and provide learning opportunities that can be applied to more business-oriented data use cases.

While all this is positive, and helps you reach the next stage of the data journey, be careful not to overpromise. Stay realistic about what can be achieved, or there will be a loss of credibility with negative consequences for the future.

EXAMPLES

One of the examples we used for communicating the power of data was a project with UNICEF on how anonymized and aggregated telco big data helped with understanding the impact of natural disasters (Telefónica 2017). We analysed the impact of an earthquake, a flood and a landslide, and showed the results using an attractive visualization. The initiative was presented at the Mobile World Congress, a major annual trade event, and received a lot of attention from the press and within our company. This definitely helped to position the data teams as creditworthy, and the collaboration with UNICEF continues.

Another example is related to air quality monitoring and prediction in large cities, such as São Paulo and Madrid. Insights generated from mobile big data helped with this monitoring, extending what can be measured by a limited number of pollution sensors (GSMA, 2018). The project was prominently featured by the mobile network industry association GSMA and in the press, creating credibility for the data teams.

CONCLUSION

The central lesson in this chapter is that in order to enhance the chances of success for data, analytics and AI teams, it's important to dedicate time and effort to communication. You can do great things, but if nobody knows about it, it's arguably less than successful. Of course, you shouldn't overpromise either. Be realistic, but by all means communicate. It is therefore very important to establish a good relationship with the Communications department of your company early on, for both internal and external publicity. If data teams are successful at this, it creates many advantages. First, it can create internal 'fans' of the data teams — people who follow their activity with interest and can act as ambassadors. Second, data professionals working in other areas might want to join the data teams, giving them the flavour of an 'extended' or 'exponential' organization (Ismail, 2014). This is very useful when the team is not allowed to grow conventionally, but can be enhanced by other people joining the effort who don't count as headcount or consume budget. Third, being well known across the organization creates demand for more data projects (use cases), helping to drive transformation from a 'data push' to a 'data pull.'

In terms of impact, I've seen projects executed in one month — using the approach outlined in this chapter — that generated more meaningful impact and awareness than others that ran for several years. The point of this chapter is not to argue that communication is more important than actually doing the work, but that it shouldn't be overlooked or left only to direct managers.

PART V

RESPONSIBILITY

In this last part of the book, I will discuss the role of data and AI in running a responsible business. There is a trend toward assigning more value to companies that, in addition to benefiting shareholders, serve the interests of other stakeholders, such as customers, employees and society at large. This is referred to as 'stakeholder capitalism' (Sundheim and Starr, 2020). As part of this, corporations are starting to look at a responsible use of data and AI.

While there is more than 15 years of experience in big data and several years in AI, the responsible use of this technology is much more recent. So, instead of being able to give concrete lessons learned, as we've done in the rest of this book, I'll focus more on practical guidelines that are emerging from this incipient, but very necessary, movement. Given the novelty of the topics, I will also briefly explain the main motivations behind them.

19. THE SOCIAL AND ETHICAL CHALLENGES OF AI AND BIG DATA

Autonomous cars use AI to learn how to drive. Once such cars are a practical reality, and on the market, they will transform the mobility ecosystem with many positive impacts. These conceivably include reduced accidents and casualties, emptier city streets and less pollution. But the same technology that enables autonomous cars also makes possible lethal autonomous weapons systems (LAWS), popularly called 'killer robots.' Through that lens, one has to ask if AI is a blessing or a curse. A specific use of deep learning, called Generative Adversarial Networks (Wikipedia, n.d.) can be used to bring back long-dead movie actors (Diamandis, 2019) or create art featuring imaginary models (Christie's, 2018). However, it also enables the creation of 'deepfakes,'[1] invented videos that depict people saying things they never said, driving the proliferation of fake news. Blessing or curse?

Deep learning has also radically improved the task of perception, both in speech and image recognition. Google Duplex[2] is able to hold a human-like dialogue to make an appointment with a hairdresser. But, that same deep learning technology applied on video also enables massive surveillance of populations in China using facial recognition, social credit scoring (Wikipedia, n.d.) and public shaming[3] of people who cross a street while the traffic light is red. Blessing or curse?

Apart from the technical capability AI is providing, its popularity is mostly due to the many positive applications that are improving our lives, in areas like medical diagnosis, automatic translation, content recommendations, business optimization, chatbots, medicine discovery and predictive maintenance, to name just a few. Yet, that same technology, in the hands of the wrong people, can also create significant harm (Brundage, 2018), in particular related to digital, physical and political security.

So far, in this book, we've shared how large organizations can enjoy the enormous positive impact of AI and big data on businesses, to improve processes, reduce costs and increase revenues. However, there are also negative side effects of using this technology at large scale. We've all heard about black box algorithms, unfair discrimination and privacy breaches. Harvard data scientist Cathy O'Neil's book, *Weapons of Math Destruction* (O'Neil, 2016), gives many examples of opaque AI decision systems with significant impact on people's lives. Amazon had to withdraw an AI system (Dastin, 2018) that treated women unfairly compared to men during the company's HR selection process. When it was introduced, the Apple Card was criticized for giving women less favourable loan conditions than men in comparable situations (Vigdor, 2019). And then there's the Cambridge Analytica debacle, where the personal information of millions of Facebook users was co-opted for political advertising (Wikipedia, n.d.). Most of these 'scandals' are not the consequence of bad intentions, but of using new technology in large business applications without giving sufficient attention to all potential risks.

From these examples, and others, we can extract a number of challenges related to the use of AI and big data.

ETHICAL AND SOCIAL CHALLENGES
OF THE USE OF AI AND BIG DATA

Much has already been written about the possible ethical and social implications associated with the use of AI and big data. Several of these implications are described and analysed in *The Myth of the Algorithm: Tales and Truths of Artificial Intelligence* (Benjamins and Salazar: 2020).

BIAS AND UNFAIR DISCRIMINATION
(SENSITIVE ATTRIBUTES)

While machine learning is able to solve complex tasks with high performance, it might use information that's undesirable from a societal or human rights perspective. For example, deciding whether to provide a loan based on race or religion is forbidden. While it's possible to remove these unwanted attributes from data sets, there are other, less obvious attributes that might correlate with these attributes — so-called proxy variables. A well-known example is the attribute 'postal code,' which might have a significant correlation with race, and in the AI model could result in discrimination. Machine learning finds whatever pattern there is in the data, regardless of specific norms and values.

Another important aspect for avoiding discrimination is whether the data set is representative of the target group with respect to variables related to protected groups. If, for example, an AI system that helps with hiring people is trained with CVs from the IT sector, you should not use that system for hiring all kinds of candidates, because in the IT sector there are significantly more men than women. As a consequence, the system could discriminate against women in its recommendations.

Apart from bias in the training data leading to possible discrimination, this can also come from the algorithm.

A machine-learning algorithm tries to be as accurate as possible when fitting the model to the training data. At the same time, all machine-learning algorithms make mistakes, providing false positives and false negatives. If the proportion of these errors is not equal for variables considered sensitive in the application (race, gender, etc.) it could result in discrimination and have a negative impact on the affected individuals. Accuracy is often defined in terms of false positives and false negatives, often through a so-called confusion matrix. But the definition of this 'accuracy' measure, whether it tries to optimize only false positives or only false negatives, or both, can have an impact on the outcome of the algorithm, and therefore on the groups of people affected by the AI program. In safety-critical domains, such as health, justice and transportation, defining 'accuracy' is not a technical decision, but a domain or even a political decision.

BLACK BOX ALGORITHM OR 'EXPLAINABILITY'

Deep learning algorithms can be highly successful, but people have a hard time understanding why they have come to a certain conclusion. As described earlier, they are proverbial 'black boxes.' For some applications, this explainability is an essential part of the decision itself, and lack of that makes the decision unacceptable. For example, a 'robo-judge' deciding on a dispute between a customer and a health insurer is unacceptable without the explanation of the decision. This is sometimes also referred to as the 'interpretability' problem. The book mentioned previously, *Weapons of Math Destruction* (O'Neil, 2016), gives many interesting examples of this.

DATA PRIVACY AND SECURITY

Big data and machine-learning systems exploit data, and many times this is personal data. As a side effect of using all this personal data, privacy might be compromised, even if unintentionally. The Cambridge Analytica scandal shows that this is a bigger issue than we might have thought (Wikipedia, n.d.).

AUTONOMOUS DECISIONS AND LIABILITY

When systems become autonomous and self-learning, accountability for their behaviour and actions becomes less obvious. In the pre-AI world, the user was accountable for incorrect usage of a device, while device failure was the manufacturer's responsibility. When systems become autonomous, and learn over time without human intervention, some behaviours will not have been foreseen by the manufacturer. It therefore becomes less clear who would be liable when something goes wrong. A clear example of this is driverless cars. Who is responsible if something goes wrong: the manufacturer, the car itself, the auto dealer or the owner? There's ongoing discussion about whether liability should be with the producer or the deployer (Committee on Legal Affairs, European Commission, 2020).

THE FUTURE OF WORK

AI can take over many boring, repetitive or dangerous tasks. But, if this happens on a massive scale, many jobs might disappear, and unemployment would skyrocket. Most experts and policymakers agree that, as with any technological revolution, jobs will be lost, new jobs will be created, and the nature of many jobs will change. Nobody knows to what extent those changes will happen, and what percentage of workers simply won't be able to make the shift to the required digital skills. In the event that fewer people are needed to maintain productivity, fewer and fewer people will work. Governments will then collect less income tax, while costs of social benefits will increase due to increased unemployment. How can this be made sustainable? Should there be a 'robot tax'? How will governments be able to pay pensions when fewer people work? Is there a need for a universal basic income (UBI) for everybody? How will the unemployed survive if AI takes many of the current jobs, and what will be their purpose in life?

DATA AND WEALTH CONCENTRATION

AI and big data are currently dominated by a few large digital companies, including the 'GAFA' giants we talked abut earlier and some Chinese mega-companies (Baidu, Alibaba, Tencent). This might lead to significant concentration of power and wealth in a few very large companies. This is mostly due to them having access to massive amounts of propriety data, which could lead to an oligopoly. Apart from the lack of competition, there is a danger that these companies keep AI as proprietary knowledge, not sharing anything with the larger society other than for the highest price possible. Another concern is that these companies could offer high-quality AI as a service, based on their data and propriety algorithms (the black box conundrum). When these AI services are used for public services, the opacity issue — no information on bias, undesirable attributes, performance, etc. — raises serious concerns. We saw this when the Los Angeles Police Department announced that it was using Amazon's 'Rekognition' face-recognition solution for policing (Brandom, 2018).

THE PEOPLE-MACHINES RELATIONSHIP

How should people relate to robots and machines? If robots become more autonomous and learn during their 'lifetime,' what sort of relationship should be allowed between robots and people? Could one's boss be a robot, or an AI system? In Asia, robots are already taking care of elderly people, offering companionship and stimulation. Could people get married to robots? One of the key aspects of such systems will be safety and security.

MALICIOUS USES

Everything mentioned above is of concern, because AI and data are applied with the intention to improve or optimize our lives. However, like any technology, AI and data can also be used with bad intentions. Think of AI-based cyber-attacks, terrorism, influencing important events with fake news, etc. (Brundage, 2018).

AI AND WARFARE

Another issue that requires attention is the application of AI for weapons and warfare, especially for LAWS armaments. Whether governments decide to use these types of applications is an explicit (political) decision, and certainly not something that will come as a surprise. Some will consider this a good use of AI, while others might call it an altogether nefarious misuse. Some organizations are already working on an international treaty to ban 'killer robots' (Delcker, 2018).

DEALING WITH THE SOCIETAL AND ETHICAL IMPACTS OF AI AND BIG DATA

It is for this reason that in the last two years many large organizations have publicly declared that they'll adhere to AI principles or ethics guidelines. Harvard University analysed the AI principles (Fjeld and Nagy, 2020) of the first 36 organizations in the world that published such guidelines. Harvard found nine categories of consideration, including human values, professional responsibility, human control, fairness & non-discrimination, transparency & explainability, safety & security, accountability, privacy and human rights. The not-for-profit organization Algorithm Watch maintains an open inventory of AI Guidelines[4] with currently over 160 organizations. And the European Commission presented its Ethics Guidelines for Trustworthy AI (HLEG, 2019) in April 2019. My company, Telefónica, published its AI Principles[5] in 2018, committing to the use of AI systems that are fair, transparent and explainable, human-centric, and with privacy & security.

These principles are an important first step toward the responsible use of AI, but principles alone are not enough. They need to be transformed into organizational processes such that they become BAU. Though initial experiences (Benjamins et al, 2019) are being shared and published (Benjamins, 2020), and there is a growing body of experience and learning, there's still a long way to go (O'Brian et al., 2020), (Newmann Cussins, 2020).

While governments need to remain vigilant for malicious use of these powerful technologies, the positive opportunities for AI and big data are enormous and will continue to grow. We believe that in the future, from a technological perspective, it will to a large extent be possible to manage and avoid the unintended, negative consequences of AI, such as bias, discrimination and opaque algorithms.

CONCLUSION

This book is about how organizations can become more data- and AI-driven, helping them capture all opportunities. But in this chapter, we've seen that there are also potential negative consequences, even though most of them will be unintended. While it is important to remain vigilant for those ethical impacts, before deciding whether to use or not use AI and big data, you should also be aware that *not* using those technologies might be worse on many levels. Therefore, not using such technology might also have an ethical implication.

In the next chapter, we will see how companies and public entities can deal with these issues in practice, to prevent and mitigate the negative impacts as much as possible. AI and big data by themselves are not bad or good, but it's the use organizations make of them that determines the impact, and that is a choice based on each organization's norms and values. Generally speaking, we can think of an ethics continuum that ranges from good to bad (Figure 19.1), and it's up to each organization to decide where it wants to be along this spectrum (Benjamins, 2020).

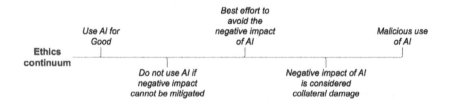

Figure 19.1 Ethics continuum of how AI can impact society

ETHICAL AND SOCIETAL
CHALLENGES OF AI

**MARCIN
DETYNIECKI**
Chief Data Scientist,
AXA Group
Associate researcher,
Sorbonne Université
Professor, Polish
Academy of Science

AI is at the root of a true revolution. It is transforming our industries and, indirectly, our society. AI is delivering the promise of a better world with applications such as cancer diagnosis, personalized and always-attentive customer service, and intelligent energy management, to name just a few. While industries go through their data & AI journey, more and more of this technology is deployed, impacting more and more people in a more or less under-controlled or autonomous way.

Although AI at scale has the potential to make our world a better one, there are some challenges along the journey. In the legal system, for example, we could imagine an AI judge that's objectively impartial and applies the law quickly and efficiently across geographies.

But, as is the case with any other new technology, AI can be misused: to perform cyberattacks, manipulate elections, create autonomous weapons, etc. And, like other new technologies, it can also have troubling side effects, such as concentration of wealth among those mastering the technology, or the unintended exclusion of others, perhaps due to a lack of historical data or access to infrastructure.

Moreover, we need to be extra careful, since AI is different in nature. In fact, we can say that what makes it 'intelligent' is that it's not explicitly programmed. Most often, algorithms learn from data. This leads to complex constructions that are not understandable by human beings. Moreover, if data has some systematic bias, the algorithm will reproduce it at scale. An AI judge trained on historical court decisions may wrongly 'learn' that those associated with a certain race or religion are predictive of recidivism.

AI is also different in its nature by mimicking human cognitive functions. This blurs the frontiers between the machine and the human, leading to possible deception or manipulation.

Because of these characteristics of AI, the need for solutions to the associated ethical and societal questions is not a trivial matter. You may think that the answer is technological — a clever pro-gramming fix to make AI 'good.' Researchers around the world are addressing the challenge, working on an AI able to explain its decisions, or able to fight bias in the data. Yet, this just a small part of the equation.

More broadly, it is about getting our data and AI journey right, meaning making the right decisions about the technology, the busi-ness, the organization and its people. It's about keeping in mind that by shaping a new world, we have the responsibility to aim for a collectively better one.

20. FROM AI PRINCIPLES TO THE RESPONSIBLE USE OF AI

In the previous chapter, we saw that many large organizations have published their ethical AI principles in the past two years, including Google,[1] IBM,[2] Microsoft,[3] Deutsche Telekom[4] and Telefónica[5] (Figure 20.1).

There are some previous examples of ethical principles being adopted for technology development, notably the IEEE Ethics Certification Program for Autonomous and Intelligent Systems.[6] And, as we saw in the previous chapter, Harvard has done a study of the ethical AI principles of 36 organizations (Fjeld et al., 2020).

Let's look specifically at Telefónica's AI Principles, published in October 2018:

- **Fair AI** means that the technology's use should not lead to discrimination based on race, ethnic origin, religion, gender, sexual orientation, disability or any other personal condition or belief. When optimizing a machine-learning algorithm for accuracy, in terms of false positives and negatives, the impact of the algorithm in the specific domain should be considered.
- **Transparent and Explainable AI** means being explicit about the kind of personal or non-personal data the AI system uses, as well as what the data is used for. When people directly interact with an AI system, that should be transparent to the users. When AI systems take, or support, decisions, a level of understanding of

how the conclusions are arrived at needs to be adequately ensured, relative to the specific application area. (It is not the same for a movie recommendation or medical diagnosis.)

- **Human-centric AI** means that it should be at the service of society and generate tangible benefits for people. AI systems should remain under human control and be driven by values-based considerations. AI used in products and services (P&S) should in no way lead to a negative impact on human rights or fall out of line with the UN's Sustainable Development Goals.
- **Privacy and Security by Design** means that when creating AI systems, which are fuelled by data, privacy and security aspects are an inherent part of the system's lifecycle.
- The principles are, by extension, also applicable when working with partners and third parties.

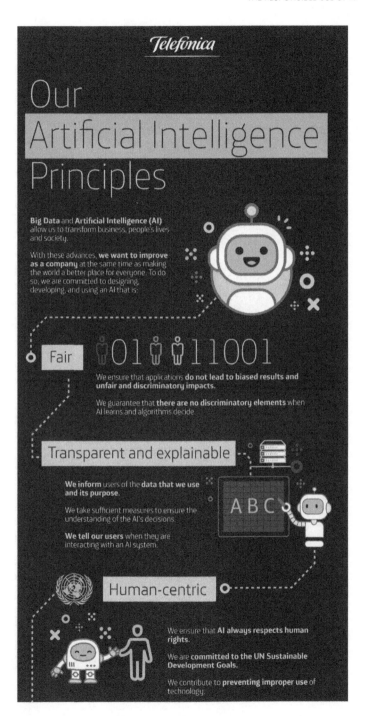

Telefónica

Our Artificial Intelligence Principles

Big Data and **Artificial Intelligence (AI)** allow us to transform business, people's lives and society.

With these advances, **we want to improve as a company** at the same time as making the world a better place for everyone. To do so, we are committed to designing, developing, and using an AI that is:

Fair

We ensure that applications **do not lead to biased results and unfair and discriminatory impacts.**

We guarantee that **there are no discriminatory elements** when AI learns and algorithms decide.

Transparent and explainable

We inform users of the **data that we use and its purpose.**

We take sufficient measures to ensure the understanding of the AI's decisions.

We tell our users when they are interacting with an AI system.

Human-centric

We ensure that **AI always respects human rights.**

We are **committed to the UN Sustainable Development Goals.**

We contribute to **preventing improper use** of technology.

231

Figure 20.1 AI Principles of Telefónica

In practice, organizations that want to commit to the responsible use of AI and big data face several challenges, including deciding what principles to adopt and how to implement them into their organizational processes.

SELECTING THE RIGHT PRINCIPLES FOR YOUR ORGANIZATION

Given the proliferation of AI principles that organizations have adopted in the past few years, it isn't obvious what guidelines it makes sense to include, and how many there should be. Figure 20.2 provides an illustration of the many AI principles organizations can choose from, related to the challenges we saw in Chapter 19. The following simple process can help to choose from the long list of principles:

- Distinguish between principles that are relevant for governments, such as the future of work, LAWS armaments, liability, concentration of power and wealth (right side of Figure 20.2), and principles that individual organizations — including private and public enterprises, public bodies, and civil societies — can act on, such as privacy, security, fairness and transparency (left side of Figure 20.2).
- Distinguish between intended and unintended consequences. Many challenges associated with the use of AI occur as an unintended side effect of the technology, such as bias, lack of explainability, the future of work, etc. (top part of Figure 20.2). Intended consequences are explicit decisions and can be controlled, such as using AI for good or for bad (bottom part of Figure 20.2). It is likely that with time, when organizations become more aware and capable of mitigating unintended consequences, those might be considered 'intended' if they continue to appear. Organizations had better formulate

their principles for the unintended consequences they can act upon (top left quadrant of Figure 20.2).

- Consider whether the AI principles cover all aspects relevant for AI systems (safety, privacy, security, fairness, etc.) in an end-to-end manner, versus covering only AI-specific challenges (fairness, explainability, human agency). There is no hard line between these categories; it is a continuum, as illustrated in Figure 20.3.

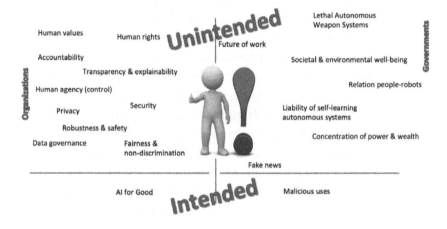

Figure 20.2 Classification of AI principles along two continuous dimensions: company-government and unintended-intended

The decisions organizations take will be partly based on the sector they operate in. For example, the aviation sector will put high value on safety associated with AI use, whereas the insurance sector will put high value on fairness, and the health sector on explainability.

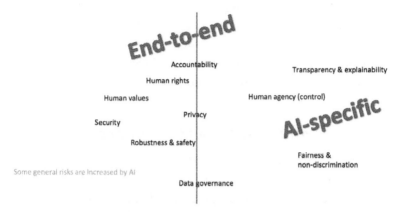

Figure 20.3 End-to-end principles versus AI-specific principles

IMPLEMENTING THE PRINCIPLES
IN YOUR ORGANIZATION

Once the principles are defined, the next step is to implement them. There is still very little published experience on the topic, but I'll take this opportunity to share Telefónica's approach. We formulated a methodology for creating Responsible AI by Design, in the tradition of Privacy and Security by Design. The methodology consists of the following ingredients:

- AI principles setting values and boundaries.
- A self-assessment questionnaire with a set of questions and recommendations, ensuring that all AI principles have been considered in the creation process.
- Tools that help answer some of the questions, and help mitigate any problems that are identified.
- Training, both technical and non-technical.
- A governance model assigning responsibilities and accountabilities.

Designing the methodology has required a cross-enterprise initiative involving different departments, such as Corporate Ethics & Sustainability, Engineering, Security, Legal, Business, IT, Human Resources and Procurement, as well as an endorsement by top management.

AN AI ETHICS QUESTIONNAIRE

For each principle, several questions are defined that must be answered by the responsible people as part of the standard product & services design methodologies. As such, we need to prepare employees, so they're able to effectively answer those questions. Some of the questions require certain understanding of AI and machine learning, so specific tools and training are required, as indicated in Figure 20.4. Depending on the answers to specific questions, recommendations may be needed to guide the employee regarding further actions. For instance, if the data set contains sensitive variables such as race, there's guidance on what needs to be done.

Principle	Question to be asked	Implemented through
Fair AI	Does your data set contain sensitive variables?	Training
	Do any of the variables strongly correlate with sensitive variables?	Technical tool
	Is/are your training data set(s) biased with respect to the target groups in case those include 'protected groups'?	Technical tool
	Is there an important impact in the specific domain of false positives (FP) and/or false negatives (FN)?	Training
	Are FP and FN unequally distributed across different (protected) groups?	Technical tool
Transparent & Explainable AI	Could the user think that s/he interacts with a person rather than with your system?	Training
	Is the AI system's outcome significantly affecting people's lives?	Training
	Do you lack sufficient understanding of how the AI-generated decisions are constructed for the domain at hand?	Training
	Could the user request an explanation for the AI-generated conclusion?	Training
	Is it difficult to be explicit about whether the data used is personal or non-personal, and about the purpose the AI system uses the data for?	Training
Human-centric AI	Is there a possibility that your P&S has a negative impact on Human Rights?	Training
	Does your P&S negatively impact the UN's SDGs?	Training
Privacy & Security by Design	Does your AI system use personal data?	Training
	Has your Privacy Impact Assessment revealed any important concerns?	Training
	In case your P&S uses anonymized data, is there an unreasonable risk of re-identification?	Technical tool
	Has your Security Assessment revealed any important concerns?	Training
Third parties	Do you need more information from your supplier to understand whether the AI module is consistent with the Principles?	Training

Figure 20.4 Each principle is operationalized through a set of questions

TECHNICAL TOOLS

Given the state of the art in this field, technical tool support is improving, but it's still limited. Therefore, for answering the majority of the questions, training is essential. Some questions call for specific training related to machine learning and AI, while others — for instance, to predict the societal impact of the application — require more general training. One category of available tools is related to checking for and mitigating unwanted bias in data sets that might lead to discrimination, and for finding 'hidden' correlations between sensitive variables (ethnicity, race, religion, etc.) and 'normal' variables (postal code, education level). There are several open source tools available, such as IBM's Fairness 360 toolkit[7] (IBM, 2018b), a tool from Pymetrics,[8] and Aequitas[9] from the University of Chicago (Benjamins et al, 2019).

Other tools are related to opening up deep-learning black box algorithms, a field referred to as Explainable AI (XAI). Such tools either try to find out what variables contribute to certain output (like SHAP[10]) or try to construct an 'external' explanation, observing all outputs and inputs and assembling a 'white box' model that is understandable (e.g. LIME[11]). Microsoft has developed an open source tool called InterpretML.[12]

TRAINING AND AWARENESS

It is important to provide training to employees that explains all relevant aspects. Training can be delivered through an online course and/or dedicated workshops with key personnel. Figure 20.5 illustrates the modules of an online course developed by Telefónica. The content of the instruction will vary depending on the technical level of employees.

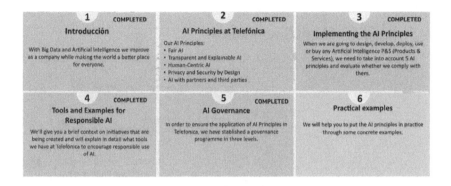

Figure 20.5 Modules of online AI ethics training course for employees

GOVERNANCE

A governance model defines responsibilities and the escalation process when the questionnaire reveals issues. Figure 20.6 shows an example of a three-step governance model for the responsible use of AI. In principle, the team responsible for the product tries to deal with all questions in the questionnaire. If they run into a problem, they escalate to a selected group of multidisciplinary experts, which at a minimum includes experts in AI, privacy and corporate ethics, and calls upon other experts as necessary. If this group can't solve the problem, it is escalated to the Responsible Business Office, which (as the name implies) meets regularly to resolve issues related to running a responsible business.

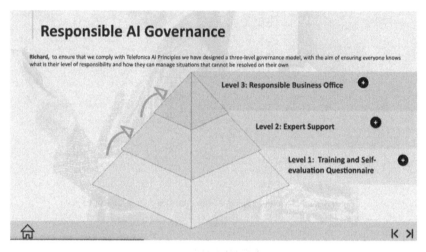

Figure 20.6 A three-step governance model for the responsible use of AI

When implementing AI principles in the organization, it might be wise to introduce a new role, called the Responsible AI Champion (RAI Champion). This person would serve as a single point of contact in every business unit for all questions related to AI and ethics. An RAI champion is knowledgeable about the area, available to fellow employees in a given geography or business unit, and provides awareness, advice, assistance and escalation if needed. Champions are also key to turning new practices into BAU processes, and as such are agents of change. An RAI Champion's specific responsibilities are to inform, educate, advise and escalate, coordinate, connect and manage change (Benjamins, 2020).

Finally, it is important to be aware that there are two types of governance: committee-based, with approvals, or on-demand, with escalation. At the early stage of AI uptake in organizations, it's been my experience that on-demand governance is a better way to start. Such an approach ensures that employees have the ability to learn, understand and fully grasp the potential impact of AI while working with it.

This promotes responsibility and is more motivational than imposing limits through controlling and approving committees. If, at some later stage, AI regulation is put in place, the organization will be well prepared for a committee-based approach because the knowledge and habits are already incorporated in the routine way of working.

AI, ON PAPER

IDOIA SALAZAR
President and
Co-founder, The
Observatory of
the Social and
Ethical Impact of AI
(OdiseIA)

The great promise of AI is already here. Every day, more companies are betting on this technology to manage their data, automate complex processes or make business predictions, based on patterns, with increasing reliability. Most of the predictions about AI point to an unprecedented revolution. For example, a comprehensive PwC report[13] indicates that by 2030, global GDP will have increased by 14% as a result of AI investment and development, which would amount to an infusion of an additional $15.7 trillion into the space. If this materializes, it would make this technology the biggest business opportunity in the mid-21st century economy.

On the other hand, economic recovery from serious crises, such as COVID-19, may also come from the use of AI systems that help develop better products, which would stimulate consumer demand. For example, better and more efficient personalization of products and services could be achieved, as well as more affordable and attractive prices for the individual consumer based on different variables that are analysed by the AI algorithm.

AI gives us the opportunity to move from an economy based on past learnings — and mistakes — to a predictive economy capable of anticipating (already with a certain degree of success) our future. On paper, the savings from the anticipation of user behaviour can run into millions of dollars. On paper, the great promises of AI can be a 'lifeboat' for many companies that, by saving costs, seek to exponentially increase their efficiency. On paper, this technology will move us to a more comfortable and better-managed world.

But, at the end of the day, all of this is just *on paper.*

ETHICS, A NECESSARY STOP ALONG THE WAY

What is becoming more and more evident, regarding the development or implementation of AI systems, is the need to take into account certain regulatory and/or ethical aspects that help to avoid a negative impact in the areas where AI is applied. The most relevant are the following:

- Respecting the data privacy of users by asking their explicit consent before using their data and sharing it with third parties.
- Preventing bias in the data and the AI algorithms. This means excluding sensitive variables, such as gender, race, sexual orientation, political ideology and others.
- Encouraging the explainability of AI algorithms. That is, making known the process that led the algorithm to make a certain decision, with the aim of promoting transparency.
- Controlling the autonomy of AI algorithms and keeping the human being at the centre. It's still the ethics of the person, not of the machine, that needs to be applied to all processes involving AI. And so, this technology must be seen as a tool — a tremendously useful one, but at the end of the day, a tool for humans. And we should not lose this humanist vision and slide into an apocalyptic and unrealistic one (at least from today's perspective) in which machines will dominate us.

So, what is needed for companies to take the next step toward ethical and responsible AI?

In a word, awareness.

We need awareness that the promise of AI on paper could be truncated by a negative impact from inadequate treatment of the peculiarities of AI systems. Awareness that the use/development of this technology implies the need for ethical thinking, if we want to reap the great possibilities it offers to us, and minimize the many potential disadvantages. Awareness that a data scientist should not be the only one involved in these ethical tasks, but that they should be supported by other interdisciplinary profiles that complement the vision of responsible and ethical use of AI algorithms and the data being used.

My organization, OdiselA,[14] was created with the objective (among others) of contributing to this awareness among public and private organizations. OdiselA works on the responsible use of AI from a sector perspective (health, education, law, defense, transport, finance, insurance, etc.); a challenges perspective (bias, explainability, liability, facial recognition, inclusive AI and more); and a transversal perspective (ethics and responsibility, training, AI tools, dissemination, legal, research and so on).

The objective is to create a great community of interdisciplinary experts that support, with their practical knowledge and their different perspectives, the expansion of AI in a responsible and ethical manner.

21. **DATA AS A FORCE FOR GOOD**

So far, we have seen how organizations can become data driven, mostly to improve their business operation, but also to create value for others so they can also become more data driven (Chapter 5). But, that same data (anonymized and aggregated) can also help to solve large problems that our societies and planet face. More and more companies are exploring this opportunity, either as a way to become more responsible or as future new business. However, companies are struggling with decision-making around all this, with little knowledge and experience on how and where to start. This chapter gives an overview of the value that privately-held data can bring to society, the challenges companies face when wanting to engage in this activity, and the wider challenges of really scaling up and creating systematic value for societies and our planet.

THE SUSTAINABLE DEVELOPMENT GOALS (SDGS)

"On September 25 2015, the United Nations adopted a set of goals to **end poverty**, **protect the planet**, and **ensure prosperity for all** as part of a new sustainable development agenda (United Nations, 2015). Each goal has specific targets to be achieved over the next 15 years. For the goals to be reached, everyone needs to do their part: governments, the private sector, civil society and people like you."[1]

The resulting 17 SDGs have 169 targets to be achieved by 2030, measured through 241 KPIs. Not all of these indicators are equally easy to measure. In March 2016, the Inter-Agency and Expert Group on SDG Indicators divided them into three tiers:

- *Tier I* comprises 98 indicators (41%) for which statistical methodologies are agreed and global data are regularly available.
- There are 50 *Tier II* indicators (21%) with clear statistical methodologies, but little available data.
- The 78 *Tier III* indicators (32%) have no agreed standards or methodology, and there is no data available.
- 15 indicators (6%) are still unclassified.

It is the responsibility of the Offices of National Statistics to monitor all 241 KPIs, and government open data is also set to play an important role. However, as we can see from the different tiers, there are still many indicators that lack data or measuring methodology. Privately-held big data from a variety of sectors can help with measuring those progress markers — in particular, data from mobile phone operators, satellite images, financial institutions or supermarkets should prove helpful. Figure 21.1 shows an overview of sectors whose privately-held data has been used for research projects contributing to the SDGs (World Bank, 2015).

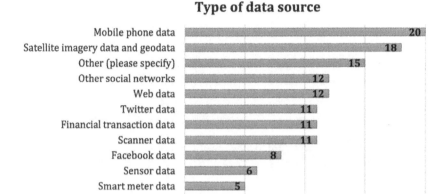

Figure 21.1 Number of research projects that use privately-held data
from specific sectors. Source: World Bank (World Bank, 2015)

Figure 21.2 shows some examples of how privately-held
big data has been used to estimate KPIs of the targets of
the SDGs. For example, payment data from financial institutions can help to estimate a consumer price index or a
poverty index. While there are official indicators to measure these indexes, they're usually difficult to execute in
rural areas of developing countries. Moreover, they often
have a very low update frequency. Search queries in Google
have been used to estimate and/or follow the propagation
of influenza outbreaks. Satellite images have been used to
estimate GDP growth through measuring man-made light
emissions. Mobile phone data has been used to estimate the
rate of illiteracy in developing countries (ratio between SMS
and calls) and to predict socio-economic levels.

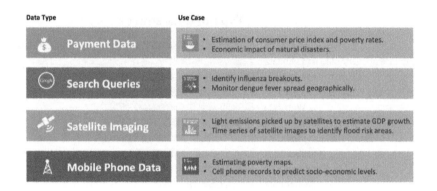

Figure 21.2 Use of privately-held data for measuring KPIs of targets of the SDGs

EXAMPLES OF PRIVATELY-HELD DATA AND THE SDGS

Below are some instances of privately-held data contributing to monitoring or achieving the SDGs.

GOAL 1: NO POVERTY. Poverty Analysis in Senegal (Orange and SUNY Buffalo).

By using mobile phone usage data and regional-level mobility information, Orange and the State University of New York's campus in Buffalo have created poverty maps showcasing a wide range of perspectives that can provide decision makers with better insights into how to eradicate poverty in Senegal in the most efficient way possible (Pokhriyal et al, 2015).

GOAL 3: GOOD HEALTH AND WELLBEING. Mobility Data Analysis in Mexico during the H1N1 Flu Outbreak (Movistar).

Scientific experts from the Telefónica R&D team used analytics on the company's data to understand the efficiency of government measures during the H1N1 flu outbreak of 2009 (Oliver, 2013), which is thought to have affected up to

375,000 people (Lipsitch, 2009). Human movement directly accelerates the spread of diseases, so they analysed mobility patterns before and after the government advised citizens to stay at home. The research revealed that only 30% stayed home, while 70% barely showed any changes in their day-to-day behaviour.

GOAL 13: CLIMATE ACTION. Using Mobile Data to Measure CO_2 Emissions in Large Cities such as São Paulo and Madrid (Telefónica).
Local governments face immense challenges associated with increased CO_2 emissions causing serious air pollution problems in cities. The Big Data for Social Good team at Telefónica used anonymized and aggregated mobility data from the mobile network to understand movement patterns of cars and predict air quality by calibrating the mobility patterns with fixed pollution sensors (AI4I, 2018).

MOBILE BIG DATA AGAINST COVID

A very recent example of using privately-held data from telecom operators can be seen in the fight against the COVID-19 pandemic. As of February 2021, the virus had infected more than 113 million people and killed more than 2.5 million worldwide. Healthcare systems are under pressure, governments are limiting free movement to control the disease's spread, economies are suffering and there will be major, long-term social consequences.

One of the main problems of COVID-19 is its (estimated) infection factor $(R_0 \cong 2.5)$,[2] which means that, on average, each infected individual infects 2.5 other people, with exponential spread as a consequence. One reason for the high infection factor is that the virus is easily transmissible through respiratory droplets, by direct contact with infected people, or by contact with contaminated objects and surfaces. All of this makes understanding population mobility and social distancing measures critically important.

Previous experience has shown that mobility insights and decision-support tools generated from anonymized and aggregated telco data can help fight pandemics. This has been demonstrated for Ebola in Africa (Wesolowski et al., 2014), Zika in Brazil[3] (Telefónica), and Swine Flu in Mexico (Oliver, 2013), to cite just a few examples. Yet, governments around the world were not prepared, from a big data perspective, to deal with COVID-19 (Oliver et al., 2020). Following a steep learning curve, many have now reached out to telecoms and are relying on mobility insights to help them manage the crisis and reboot shut-down economic activity.

The European Commission is analysing anonymized and aggregated telco big data (JRC 2020) in order to:

- Understand the spatial dynamics of epidemics using historical matrices of national and international mobility flows. (Mobility patterns might help predict early virus propagation.)
- Quantify the impact of physical distancing measures on mobility, including the phasing out of such measures as appropriate. (Monitoring of population movement restrictions and their incremental relaxation.)
- Feed epidemiological models, to help evaluate the effects of physical distancing measures on reducing the rate of virus spread. (Improve epidemiological models for virus propagation.)
- Feed models to estimate the economic costs of the different interventions. (Monitoring recovery of economic activity.)

As an example of the EC's work, Figure 21.3 shows the change in mobility at province level in 15 European countries

(Santamaria et al., 2020). The map on the left shows the reduction in total mobility between 28 February and 3 April of 2020, when mobility in Europe was at its lowest pandemic period level. The map on the right provides a comparative view of between 28 February and 29 May of that year, when mobility had already recovered because of lifted lockdowns in some areas. It's also clear from the maps that in some countries (Austria, for instance) mobility had changed in a spatially non-uniform way, emphasizing the value of data at a sub-national level.

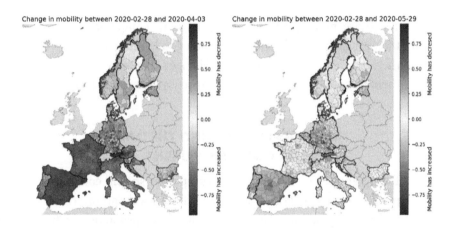

Figure 21.3 Change in mobility between 28 February and 3 April 2020 (left) and between 28 February and 29 May of that year (right). Reprinted with permission.

It should be clear by now that there is great social value in privately-held data. It's therefore no surprise that more companies are considering joining this movement. Indeed, more and more intermediate organizations have become active in this space, helping companies join the Govlab of NYU, UN Global Pulse, UNICEF, the World Bank's data initiative, etc. This trend is also reflected in the EC's European Data Strategy,[4] the final report of the

Expert Group on Business to Government Data Sharing,[5] and the European Green Deal.[6]

In the next section we will discuss the sorts of considerations companies typically work through when taking this decision.

COMPANY CONSIDERATIONS FOR JOINING THE DATA FOR GOOD MOVEMENT

There are many positives associated with companies using their privately-held data for the greater good. At the same time, there are also some very real challenges that may dissuade them from doing so. Below we will discuss the pros and cons.

REASONS FOR JOINING THE DATA FOR GOOD MOVEMENT

Doing good. The main reasons companies should consider participating is that they actually can do good and improve the world by helping solve some of its major problems, such as hunger, climate change, equality, etc. This is detailed in the SDGs.

Innovation and know-how. Such projects usually require new ways of collaboration and new technologies, which give companies an opportunity to experiment without direct commercial risks. Many start by applying data and analytics to improve their internal business, and data for good then allows them to explore new business opportunities by leveraging their first-party data externally. It also helps companies strengthen their privacy knowledge and practices, because external data sharing requires even stronger measures than internal data use.

Access to governments. Data for good projects usually benefit governments, even though they might be executed through humanitarian organizations. Many of the initiatives provide direct access to policymakers in local, regional and central governments, which helps companies position themselves as responsible players, while helping them open up new business opportunities.

Strengthening of brand and reputation. Closely working together in data and AI projects with renowned humanitarian organizations strengthens companies' positioning as responsible businesses.

Business opportunity. Although the majority of data for good projects are philanthropic in nature, sometimes they enable the recovery of at least the incurred costs. This is primarily happening through funding from philanthropic organizations, such as the Bill & Melinda Gates Foundation.

Employee engagement. Having a social purpose, apart from pure commercial objectives, is increasingly important for external reputation but especially for employees. Employees value their organization's social initiatives, such as those related to the UN SDGs, particularly if they're hands-on rather than just providing funds to an NGO.

REASONS FOR NOT JOINING THE DATA FOR GOOD MOVEMENT

While there are many good reasons to start sharing privately-held data for social purposes, there are also factors that may make companies reluctant to embark on this journey.

Privacy & Security. Almost all data sharing is based on anonymized and aggregated data. While there are good anonymization techniques available, which can be coupled with additional privacy enhancing technologies — and while in practice it's almost impossible to re-identify individuals — anonymization is in theory never 100% possible.

Moreover, data sharing for good almost always requires that the data leave the organization, and move outside its control, which implies a risk (at least a psychological one). In addition, data that leaves the company might be combined and cross-referenced with other data sources, which increases the theoretical risk of re-identification. These questions, especially for companies that are new in the field of data sharing, create stress for the legal, privacy and security departments.

Legal. For many companies, most of the relevant anonymized and aggregated data originates from customer data. There is not always full consensus on whether sharing data externally, or moving it to other countries or continents, is allowed. Organizations also face the challenges of complying with a wide range of data protection regulations in the different countries where they operate.

Corporate reputation. Even though sharing anonymized and aggregated data would normally improve a company's reputation, in some cases there might be a negative impact. If, in the end, it is shared beyond its original purposes, and if there's a data breach, this might have a negative reputational impact. There's also persistent misunderstanding of what is actually anonymized data, versus personal data. The media and politicians have been known to confuse the two, and generate negative noise. Finally, most data-driven decisions based on privately-held data aim to improve the lot of the vulnerable parts of society, but this may have a perceived negative impact on more affluent and influential demographics. This is something that companies are usually not comfortable with.

Big data is a new strategic asset. Businesses might also struggle with strategic commercial issues. Many companies have only just learned that big data is a key asset, so they may wonder why they'd want to share it, even if for the greater good. And, they might ask, why share it for free?

Confidential information. Companies might wonder whether the competition could get hold of their data assets and — even if it's anonymized and aggregated — potentially make strategic use of it. They might prefer not to incur this risk, even if it's a remote possibility.

Cannibalization. Sharing data for good mostly happens today on a philanthropic basis, and sometimes with governments. But governments are also customers of many companies' services. Does this mean that sharing data for social good cannibalizes some of these companies' external big data revenue — for instance, constricting big-ticket government revenue streams? Could a big data for social good project jeopardize other existing business opportunities?

HOW AND WHERE TO START

As we have seen, there are compelling reasons to start with sharing big data for social good, but there are also uncertainties that may make companies reluctant to join in. When brave companies finally decide to initiate this activity, what should they think about and how should they start?

Several decisions have to be made up front, and while they will be presented here separately, there might be interdependencies.

WHERE TO LOCATE THE DEPARTMENT WITHIN THE ORGANIZATION

The most frequently used approaches I've seen for organizational positioning are:

* **As part of a business unit.** Some companies have a big data business unit that delivers products and services to

B2B customers. This unit is already equipped with the capability to share data in a secure, privacy-preserving way, so many of the possible concerns are already taken care of. The business unit may create a small new department that is focused on social good projects. This was the option chosen by Telefónica in 2016. As we will see, this choice has a direct impact on the financing decision.

- **As part of a research department.** Given that most of the social good activity is new for many companies, it is not uncommon to create a small group as part of the research area. R&D typically has the flexibility to deal with new technology and is used to collaborating externally, with different types of organizations. And, because many of the social good projects start with pilots, the research function is a perfect place for that.

- **As part of the Chief Data Office area.** This is the place where all data is collected, stored, curated and securely made available to the rest of the organization, and possibly also externally (see Chapter 5). Moreover, many CDO teams also include analytics or AI areas, to create value from data. The CDO is therefore a natural place to host the new big data for good area, as it includes all prime material and technical expertise, not only from a data perspective, but also concerning privacy and security.

While these are the most popular options, an alternative is to create the department as part of the **Sustainability** or **Corporate Social Responsibility** (CSR) area. Many social good projects take place in collaboration with humanitarian organizations, NGOs or philanthropists, and it's the Sustainability or CSR department that owns those relationships and partnerships. Setting up the data for good team in this area helps foster early engagement with major external players, which can give the initiative an initial boost.

HOW TO FINANCE YOUR DATA
FOR GOOD ACTIVITIES

Meanwhile, there are different options for financing the data for good activities, and we will discuss the most common ones. However, it's important to note that these financing schemes are not mutually exclusive. On the contrary, they can work perfectly together, and many successful data for good areas do exactly that, independent of where the team sits organizationally.

- **Financed by a business unit.** In this case, which happens most often when the data for good team sits in a business unit, costs are covered by the unit, increasing the business's operational cost and headcount. This is feasible if the business unit is of a certain size. For instance, a small data for good team would require a business unit of over 100 people. To some extent, the business unit can view it as a marketing expense, because the social projects help strategically position the company with governments and other public bodies. Moreover, successful pilot projects might turn into new contracts. Another advantage is that the cannibalization problem discussed in the previous section can be dealt with swiftly, because both activities are part of the same area. As such, the direct manager can immediately resolve any potential issue without a long escalation process. The main advantage of this model is that there's a direct route from the activity to the market, in the event that there exists a market for these kinds of projects.

- **Financed by Research.** Many large companies have dedicated research areas, which are financed by innovation funds and external research funding from governmental institutions. For a large research area, it takes little effort to include a small new data for good team. The main disadvantage is that there's a risk that the focus of the projects is more on research (generation of knowledge, patents and academic publications) than on bringing the results to society, to do real good on the ground.

- **Financed by the Sustainability or CSR area.** These areas usually have budgets for collaborating with NGOs and humanitarian organizations. When a company decides to set up a new data for good initiative, this opens up for the CSR team a completely new way of collaboration with its stakeholders. And, in my experience, the CSR area embraces this new way. Instead of 'just' providing donations and effort, the CSR team can now also engage in hands-on technical work to bring the collaboration to life. For example, in the telecom sector, rather than donating money to an NGO whose goal is to assist victims of forced migration, through data for good it can offer a map with population-movement flows and concentrations, helping the NGO be more precise in its operations. To make this so, the CSR area could fund part of the data for good project. In my experience, this is really a win-win-win, where all stakeholders (NGO, CSR and data for good) benefit in a positive spiral.

- **Financed by external funding.** Today there are also many specific funds, either from local, regional, national or international governments, or from large philanthropists or NGOs. These types of financing are important, especially when the data for good area is already up and running. However, they're less appropriate as a source of initial funds to set up the area, because they take time to materialize.

- **Financed as a business by customers.** This would be one of the best ways to finance data for good activities. Indeed, data for good projects, when put into operation, can deliver significant improvements and operational cost savings for governments, NGOs and humanitarian organizations. However, at present, this type of financing is only happening at a very small scale. Most governments and humanitarian organizations expect corporate data for good initiatives for free, provided on a pro bono basis. We'll look at that later in this chapter.

HOW TO STRUCTURE THE DATA FOR GOOD TEAM

Once there is a place in the organization and budget for the new data for good area, there are other relevant aspects to take into account for a good functioning area. The following are some of those considerations:

- **Data steward role.** Apart from the technical data work to be performed — including data engineering, data science and data visualization — coordination with different parts of the company is critical. This includes cooperation between CSR/Sustainability, Reputation, Legal & Privacy, Security, Research and Business. Moreover, the area also needs to build and maintain excellent relationships with relevant external organizations, including governments at all levels, humanitarian organizations and other NGOs. In most companies today, there's no dedicated role to take care of all of that in a coordinated way, and progress depends above all on specific individuals with passion for making data for good projects work. Both New York University's Govlab (Verhulst et al., 2020) and the EC's Expert Group on Business-to-Government Data Sharing (Expert Group on B2G Data Sharing, 2020) recommend creation of a new organizational role whose responsibility is to take care of this coordination process in a coherent way. A 'data steward' would also make it clear, for external relationships, who to contact in the organization regarding data for good projects. Unfortunately, external parties today find themselves having to contact whoever will listen, and usually end up in many repetitive, often fruitless meetings with people from all kinds of departments (CSR, AI, CDO, Privacy, Legal, etc.).

- **Technical data team.** Data for good projects involve hands-on activities with real data. Therefore, the team must have several technical profiles.
- **Local support from the operating business.** While data for good teams are usually set up at headquarters, many of the projects will be executed with local businesses in specific geographies. It's therefore critical to identify the right people and areas in those local businesses. If local data is needed, a relationship with the local CDO is needed. If the collaboration is with the local part of a global humanitarian organization, the local CSR area that takes care of institutional relationships needs to be included. And, if there's a follow-up business opportunity after the data for good project, the business area needs to be involved.

THE CURRENT STATE OF DATA FOR GOOD, AND HOW TO MOVE FORWARD

The data for good movement has grown significantly over the last few years, and there are now many companies active in the area. Moreover, multiple facilitating organizations are trying to scale the activity around the world. Unfortunately, most of this remains limited to pilots or prototypes. A pilot typically demonstrates that a historically documented problem area can be addressed using privately-held data. For instance, the impact of a natural disaster like an earthquake is investigated using a data set specifically extracted for the research. Or, a pilot shows that there is a significant correlation between mobility data generated by telco network data and the spread of a pandemic. These results mean that for a next earthquake or pandemic, if the pilots were turned into operational systems, the impact of the earthquake's damage could be reduced, and the spread of the pandemic could be predicted such that preventative measures could be better targeted.

However, as of 2020, very few such operational systems exist. This has been especially evident with the COVID-19 pandemic, with governments around the world struggling to use modern technologies to manage and control lockdowns and other restrictions to limit the virus's spread (Oliver et al., 2020). However, a report by the EC's Expert Group on B2G Data Sharing (Expert Group on B2G Data Sharing, 2020) makes it clear that the sharing of privately-held data for the public good is still in its infancy.

Organizations that actively promote data for good initiatives and try to scale them up include the GSMA's AI for Impact (AI4I) task force,[7] the Global Partnership for Sustainable Development Data (GP4SDD),[8] the World Bank's initiative on Data for Better Lives (World Bank, 2020) and NYU's Govlab.[9]

One of the main reasons many data for good initiatives do not outlive the pilot phase is the lack of a financially sustainable model. Governments have shown little interest in procuring such systems, and often lack the digital maturity to understand their full impact. Humanitarian organizations expect donations from large corporations, rather than funding them for executing data for good projects, even if such projects would allow the organization to save a significant amount. Finally, the truth is that companies are not in the business of philanthropy. They're willing to spend a certain amount to demonstrate the feasibility of the projects, but running an operational system requires infrastructure, a team and a budget. At the time of writing, this is still a challenge that needs to be solved before data for good projects will solve real problems in the world.

THE POWER OF TELCO DATA AND AI TO UNDERSTAND INTERNAL FORCED DISPLACEMENTS

PEDRO A. DE ALARCÓN, PhD
Data Scientist and Head of Big Data for Social Good
(Telefónica)

There is an urgent need for more accurate, timely and comprehensive data to make the SDGs an actionable framework for sustainable development that can drive policies and programs in real time, for all people. Infectious diseases like COVID-19, pollution, earthquakes, floods and other disasters are among the greatest challenges the world faces today. Among them, forced internal displacement (FID) — due to armed conflict, generalized violence, human rights violations and other factors — is quickly becoming a silent world crisis. As of the end of 2019, 50.8 million people were displaced from their homes and forced to move elsewhere in their country, in order to survive.[10]

Data on FIDs is inherently difficult to collect. This is particularly the case in low- and middle-income countries, where the displaced are more likely to live in remote locations with poor infrastructure, or may be surrounded by volatile security situations. Thus, measuring migration patterns becomes a very complex task, compounding the economic and social impact on these individuals, families and communities.

The potential of telco data in migration analysis resides in two factors. Due to the high penetration of mobile phones, it allows working with massive data samples, much higher than the volume used in survey-based analysis. On the other hand, due to the digitization of connectivity, high-quality data is systematically generated. The rich nature of telco data allows the determination of probable places of residence (and changes in them), insights from the network of contacts (social network analysis) and other relevant information related to the subscriber (service top-ups, type of contract, etc.). In addition, all this information is used with sufficient guarantees of information security, anonymity and aggregation, as it is a regulated sector in accordance with the legislation of each country.

However, the main technical problem is how to infer that a mobile line corresponds to a displaced or migrant person. From a machine-learning point of view, this should ideally be a **supervised** problem. In other words, a large group of people was available who were clearly displaced individuals. This training set is the basis for the algorithms to learn and the mobility patterns, calls, geographic factors, etc., associated to FIDs. That would allow estimating the total mass of migrants vis-à-vis the rest of the uncharacterized individuals. Such an approach is the most appropriate but requires close collaboration between governments and the private sector, guaranteeing maximum protection for those affected, since personal information must be crossed at the individual level. As a notable example, we can mention the data set created for the Data for Refugee Challenge, which studies migratory movements of Syrian refugees in Turkey.[11]

Another approach to quantify migrations consists of integrating aggregated data sources of public and private origin, in which each source reports aggregated figures. It is expected that the integration of such data sources, when aggregated, produces higher quality estimates than the individual sources on their own. For example, IMMAP[12] has generated monitoring reports of Venezuelans displaced to Colombia using aggregated data from Facebook (through an ingenious use of its ad campaign tool) together with official statistics reported by the Colombian government. In another notable case, Telefónica's Big Data for Social Good team, together with the UN's Food and Agriculture Organization (FAO), addressed the problem of migration caused by climate change in La Guajira, a region in northern Colombia, which has suffered long periods of drought for years.[13] To do this, they analysed the changes of residence patterns of tens of thousands of mobile lines, detecting permanent movements from different cities in La Guajira to large cities such as Medellín, Bogotá or Cali. Once the methodology is deployed, it's relatively easy to scale it by means of analytics, so insights could be constantly updated.

These examples illustrate the great potential of data to improve understanding of the global phenomenon of forced displacement, which can help protect and meet the needs of these people. However, important challenges remain. First, public-private partnerships are key, to maximize the potential of the data and to guarantee sustainable investment for the long term. Second, ethical aspects must be taken into account and evaluated, since the same tools can be used for totally opposite purposes, such as persecution of the displaced.

ENDNOTES

ACKNOWLEDGEMENTS

1. Experts appear in reversed alphabetical order of the first name

INTRODUCTION

1. OSS: Operating Support Systems, BSS: Business Support Systems

CHAPTER 1

1. If the CDO is placed at CEO-1, this means a direct reporting line. If the CDO is placed at CEO-2, this means that there is one line manager between the CEO and the CDO, etc.

CHAPTER 4

1. https://data-speaks.luca-d3.com/2017/12/brazilian-cities-urban-planning-with-data.html

2. https://data-speaks.luca-d3.com/2017/10/planning-retail-sites-big-data.html

3. https://data-speaks.luca-d3.com/2017/10/peru-tourism-big-data.html

CHAPTER 7

1. https://ec.europa.eu/info/strategy/priorities-2019-2024/europe-fit-digital-age/european-data-strategy_en

CHAPTER 9

1. European Data Portal (2020), 'The Economic Impact of Open Data: Opportunities for value creation in Europe', https://www.europeandataportal.eu/sites/default/files/the-economic-impact-of-open-data.pdf

2. The Open Data Institute (2020), "Case study: The value of sharing data to build trust", https://theodi.org/article/case-study-the-value-of-sharing-data-to-build-trust/

3. The Open Data Institute (2020), "Case study: The value of sharing data for improving market reach", https://theodi.org/article/case-study-the-value-of-sharing-data-for-improving-market-reach/

4. The Open Data Institute (2015), "Thomson Reuters' data services go open", https://theodi.org/project/open-enterprise-case-study-thomson-reuters/

5. The Open Data Institute (2018), "How Facebook, Apple and Microsoft are contributing to an openly licensed map of the world", https://theodi.org/article/how-are-facebook-apple-and-microsoft-contributing-to-openstreetmap/

6. Lloyd's Register Foundation (2019), 'Insight report on sharing engineering data', https://www.lrfoundation.org.uk/en/news/insight-report-on-data/

7. The Open Data Institute (2020), 'Data sharing in the private sector', https://theodi.org/service/business-data-sharing/

CHAPTER 10

1. https://www.digitalxborder.com/

2. https://bigml.com/

CHAPTER 13

1. A French multinational electric utility company, headquartered near Paris, that's active in energy transition, electricity generation and distribution, natural gas, nuclear power, renewable energy and petroleum.

CHAPTER 15

1. https://www.Telefónica.com/en/web/press-office/-/Telefónica-strengthens-its-big-data-capabilities-with-the-integration-of-synergic-partners

CHAPTER 17

1. https://bigml.com/

2. https://bigml.com/

CHAPTER 19

1. https://www.youtube.com/watch?v=cQ54GDm1eL0&feature=youtu.be

2. https://www.youtube.com/watch?v=D5VN56jQMWM

3. https://www.youtube.com/watch?v=VJOrlZsNHf4

4. https://inventory.algorithmwatch.org/

5. https://www.Telefónica.com/en/web/responsible-business/our-commitments/ai-principles

CHAPTER 20

1. https://www.blog.google/technology/ai/ai-principles/

2. https://www.zdnet.com/article/ibms-rometty-lays-out-ai-considerations-ethical-principles/

3. https://www.microsoft.com/en-us/ai/responsible-ai?activetab=pivot1%3aprimaryr6

4. https://www.telekom.com/en/company/digital-responsibility/digital-ethics-deutsche-telekoms-ai-guideline

5. https://www.Telefónica.com/en/web/responsible-business/our-commitments/ai-principles

6. https://standards.ieee.org/industry-connections/ecpais.html

7. https://aif360.mybluemix.net/

8. https://github.com/pymetrics/audit-ai

9. https://github.com/dssg/aequitas

10. https://shap.readthedocs.io/en/latest/

11. https://github.com/marcotcr/lime

12. https://interpret.ml/

13. https://www.pwc.com/gx/en/issues/data-and-analytics/publications/artificial-intelligence-study.html

14. https://www.odiseia.org/

CHAPTER 21

1. http://www.un.org/sustainabledevelopment/sustainable-development-goals/

2. https://www.weforum.org/agenda/2020/05/covid-19-what-is-the-r-number/

3. https://elpais.com/elpais/2018/10/29/planeta_futuro/1540825274_349206.html

4. https://ec.europa.eu/info/strategy/priorities-2019-2024/europe-fit-digital-age/european-data-strategy_en

5. https://ec.europa.eu/digital-single-market/en/news/experts-say-privately-held-data-available-european-union-should-be-used-better-and-more

6. https://ec.europa.eu/info/strategy/priorities-2019-2024/european-green-deal_en

7. https://aiforimpacttoolkit.gsma.com/realising-scale/the-big-data-for-social-good-initiative

8. https://www.data4sdgs.org/

9. https://www.thegovlab.org/

10. iDMC. Global Report on Internal Displacement 2020. https://www.internal-displacement.org/global-report/grid2020/

11. Data for Refugees: The D4R Challenge on Mobility of Syrian Refugees in Turkey. https://www.researchgate.net/publication/326144689_Data_for_Refugees_The_D4R_Challenge_on_Mobility_of_Syrian_Refugees_in_Turkey

12. iMMAP Report: Tracking Venezuelan Refugee, Migrant, and Returnee Populations in Colombia through Facebook. https://immap.org/news/immap-report-tracking-venezuelan-refugee-migrant-and-returnee-populations-in-colombia-through-facebook/

13. GSMA. Building communities resilient to climate extremes. https://aiforimpacttoolkit.gsma.com/resources/Big-Data-for-Social-Good_TEF_FAO_Case_Study.pdf

BIBLIOGRAPHY

INTRODUCTION

Manyika, J., M. Chui, B. Brown, J. Bughin, R. Dobbs, C. Roxburgh and A Hung Byers. May 2011. "Big Data: The Next Frontier for Innovation, Competition, and Productivity." https://www. mckinsey.com/business-functions/mckinsey-digital/our-insights/ big-data-the-next-frontier-for-innovation.

Bean, R. and T.H. Davenport. 5 February 2019. "Companies Are Failing in Their Efforts to Become Data-Driven." https://hbr.org/2019/02/ companies-are-failing-in-their-efforts-to-become-data-driven.

CHAPTER 1

Davenport, T.H. and B. Randy. 7 February 2020. "Are You Asking Too Much of Your Chief Data Officer?" *Harvard Business Review.* https://hbr.org/2020/02/are-you-asking-too-much-of-your-chief-data-officer.

Gartner. 11 February 2016. "Gartner Identifies Four Types of Chief Data Officer Organization." https://www.gartner.com/en/newsroom/ press-releases/2016-02-11-gartner-identifies-four-types-of-chief-data-officer-organization.

NewVantage Partners. 2021. "NewVantage Partners." *Big Data and AI Executive Survey 2021.* https://c6abb8db-514c-4f5b-b5a1-fc710f1e464e.filesusr.com/ugd/ e5361a_76709448ddc6490981f0cbea42d51508.pdf.

Zaidi, J. 2 October 2015. "Some CDOs are Thriving While Others Are Departing - Here's Why?" https://www.linkedin.com/pulse/heres-why-some-cdos-thriving-while-others-departing-jay-zaidi/.

CHAPTER 2

Altimetrik. 2015. "Achieving Enterprise Agility through Bimodal Transformation." https://www.gartner.com/imagesrv/media-products/pdf/ALTIMETRIK/Altimetrik-1-354WZ5A.pdf.

CHAPTER 3

Henke, N., J. Bughin, M. Chui, J. Manyika, T. Saleh, B. Wiseman, and G. Sethupathy. December 2016. "The Age of Analytics: Competing in a Data-driven World." *McKinsey Global Institute*. https://www. mckinsey.com/~/media/McKinsey/Industries/Public%20and%20 Social%20Sector/Our%20Insights/The%20age%20of%20analytics%20 Competing%20in%20a%20data%20driven%20world/MGI-The-Age-of-Analytics-Full-report.pdf.

Manyika et al. May 2011. op. cit.

Bughin, J., E. Hazan, S. Ramaswamy, M. Chui, T. Allas, P. Dahlström, N. Henke, and M. Trench. June 2017. "Artificial Intelligence: The Next Digital Frontier?" *McKinsey Global Institute*. https://www.mckinsey. com/~/media/mckinsey/industries/advanced%20electronics/our%20 insights/how%20artificial%20intelligence%20can%20deliver%20 real%20value%20to%20companies/mgi-artificial-intelligence-discussion-paper.ashx.

Davenport, T. H. and Patil, D. J. October 2012. "Data Scientist: The Sexiest Job of the 21st Century." *Harvard Business Review*. https://hbr. org/2012/10/data-scientist-the-sexiest-job-of-the-21st-century.

CHAPTER 5

European Commission. 19 February 2020. "A European Strategy for Data." https://ec.europa.eu/info/sites/info/files/communication-european-strategy-data-19feb2020_en.pdf.

CHAPTER 6

Wikipedia. n.d. "Ansoff Matrix." *Wikipedia*. https://en.wikipedia.org/wiki/ Ansoff_Matrix.

TMForum. 2015. "GB979A Big Data Analytics Use Cases R15.0.1." https:// www.tmforum.org/resources/standard/gb979a-big-data-analytics-use-cases-r15-0-1/.

Bughin et al. June 2017. op. cit.

Rao, A.S. and G. Verweij. 2019. "Sizing the Prize: What's the Real Value of AI For your Business and How Can you Capitalise?" *PWC*. https://www. pwc.com/gx/en/issues/analytics/assets/pwc-ai-analysis-sizing-the-prize-report.pdf.

SDA Bocconi. 2019. "Automation Opportunity Matrix." *Reply*. http://www. reply.com/en/data-robotics-automation-opportunity-matrix.

CHAPTER 7

Hadoop. 2020. "Apache Hadoop." http://hadoop.apache.org/.

Henke et al. December 2016. op. cit.

Manyika et al. May 2011. op. cit.

Press, G. 2 January 2017. "6 Predictions For The $203 Billion Big Data Analytics Market." *Forbes*. https://www.forbes.com/sites/gilpress/2017/01/20/6-predictions-for-the-203-billion-big-data-analytics-market/#1c7a8edc2083.

CHAPTER 9

Manyika, J., M. Chui, D. Farrell, S. Van Kuiken, P. Groves, and E. Almasi Doshi. 2013. "Open Data: Unlocking Innovation and Performance with Liquid Information." *McKinsey Global Institute*. https://www.mckinsey.com/business-functions/mckinsey-digital/our-insights/open-data-unlocking-innovation-and-performance-with-liquid-information#.

Berners-Lee, T. 2012. "5 ★ OPEN DATA." https://5stardata.info/en/.

European Commission. 2019. "From the Public Sector Information (PSI) Directive to the Open Data Directive." *Shaping Europe's digital future*. https://ec.europa.eu/digital-single-market/en/public-sector-information-psi-directive-open-data-directive.

Wikipedia. n.d. "Open data." *Wikipedia*. https://en.wikipedia.org/wiki/Open_data.

CHAPTER 11

Carr, N. 2008. *The Big Switch: Rewiring the World, from Edison to Google*. New York: W. W. Norton & Company.

Chapel, J. DZone. 1 April 2020. "Who Is Leading Among The Big Three?: AWS vs. Azure vs. Google Cloud Market Comparison." https://dzone.com/articles/who-is-leading-among-the-big-three-aws-vs-azure-vs.

Mariani, D. 2019. "Bimodal Analytics: What Modern DataOps Teams Need to Know When Choosing their Analytics Platform Mix." https://www.itproportal.com/features/bimodal-analytics-what-modern-dataops-teams-need-to-know-when-choosing-their-analytics-platform-mix/.

Shu, X, K. Tian, A. Ciambrone, and D. Yao. 18 January 2017. "Breaking the Target: An Analysis of Target Data Breach and Lessons Learned." https://arxiv.org/abs/1701.04940.

CHAPTER 14

Chong, D. 30 April 2020. Towards Data Science. "Deep Dive into Netflix's Recommender System." https://towardsdatascience.com/deep-dive-into-netflixs-recommender-system-341806ae3b48.

Croll, A. and B. Yoskovitz. 2013. *Lean Analytics, Use Data to Build a Better Startup Faster.* http://leananalyticsbook.com/. O'Reilly Media.

Davies, A. 2019. "How Big Data Helped Netflix Series House of Cards Become a Blockbuster?" *Sofy.* https://sofy.tv/blog/big-data-helped-netflix-series-house-cards-become-blockbuster/.

Open Data Institute. 3 November 2017. "What is 'Open Data' and Why Should we Care?" *ODI.* https://theodi.org/article/what-is-open-data-and-why-should-we-care/.

Paulina. 7 March 2017. "1st, 2nd and 3rd Party Data – What It All Means?" *Adsquare.* https://www.adsquare.com/1st-2nd-and-3rd-party-data-what-it-all-means/#:~:text=In%20general%2C%20the%20.

Smith, D. 6 September 2019. "The Exponential Growth of Big Data." *Tweak Your Biz.* https://tweakyourbiz.com/growth/productivity/big-data-growth.

PART IV

Benjamins, R. and I. Salazar. 2020. *The Myth of the Algorithm: Tales and Truths of Artificial Intelligence (in Spanish).* Madrid: Anaya Multimedia.

CHAPTER 17

McNellis, J. 5 November 2019. "You're Likely Investing a Lot in Marketing Analytics, but Are You Getting the Right Insights?" https://blogs.gartner.com/jason-mcnellis/2019/11/05/youre-likely-investing-lot-marketing-analytics-getting-right-insights/.

Croll, A. and B. Yoskovitz. 2013. op. cit.

CHAPTER 18

GSMA. 2018. "Predicting Air Pollution Levels 24 to 48 Hours in Advance in São Paulo, Brazil." https://aiforimpacttoolkit.gsma.com/resources/Big-Data-for-Social-Good_TEF_Brazil_Case-Study.pdf.

Ismail, S. 2014. *Exponential Organizations: Why new organizations are ten times better, faster, and cheaper than yours (and what to do about it).* New York: Diversion Books.

Telefónica. 2017. "Telefónica Joins UNICEF's "Magic Box" Initiative to Drive the Use of Big Data for Social Good." https://www.Telefónica.com/en/web/press-office/-/Telefónica-joins-unicef-s-magic-box-initiative-to-drive-the-use-of-big-data-for-social-good.

United Nations. 2015. "Sustainable Development Goals." https://www.un.org/sustainabledevelopment/sustainable-development-goals/.

PART V

Sundheim, D. and K. Starr. 22 January 2020. "Making Stakeholder Capitalism a Reality." *Harvard Business Review Home*. https://hbr.org/2020/01/making-stakeholder-capitalism-a-reality.

CHAPTER 19

O'Neil, C. 2016. *Weapons of Math Destruction: How Big Data Increases Inequality and Threatens Democracy*. Crown Books.

Committee on Legal Affairs, European Commission. 27 April 2020. "DRAFT REPORT with recommendations to the Commission on a Civil liability regime for AI." *European Parliament*. https://www.europarl.europa.eu/doceo/document/JURI-PR-650556_EN.pdf.

Brandom, R. 22 May 2018. "Amazon is Selling Police Departments a Real-time Facial Recognition System." *The Verge*. https://www.theverge.com/2018/5/22/17379968/amazon-rekognition-facial-recognition-surveillance-aclu.

Delcker, J. 28 March 2018. "France, Germany under fire for failing to back 'killer robots' ban." *Politico*. https://www.politico.eu/article/artificial-intelligence-killer-robots-france-germany-under-fire-for-failing-to-back-robots-ban/.

Diamandis, P. H. 3 May 2019. "AI Is About to Completely Change the Face of Entertainment." *Singularity Hub*. https://singularityhub.com/2019/05/03/ai-is-about-to-completely-change-the-face-of-entertainment/.

Christie's. 2018. "Is Artificial Intelligence Set to Become Art's Next Medium?" *Christie's*. https://www.christies.com/features/A-collaboration-between-two-artists-one-human-one-a-machine-9332-1.aspx.

Brundage, M. February 2018. *The Malicious Use of Artificial Intelligence: Forecasting, Prevention, and Mitigation*. https://arxiv.org/pdf/1802.07228.pdf.

Dastin, J. 11 October 2018. "Amazon Scraps Secret AI Recruiting Tool that Showed Bias Against Women." *Reuters.* https://www.reuters.com/article/us-amazon-com-jobs-automation-insight/amazon-scraps-secret-ai-recruiting-tool-that-showed-bias-against-women-idUSKCN1MK08G.

Vigdor, N. 10 November 2019. "Apple Card Investigated After Gender Discrimination Complaints." *The New York Times.* https://www.nytimes.com/2019/11/10/business/Apple-credit-card-investigation.html.

Fjeld, J. and A. Nagy. 15 january 2020. "Principled Artificial Intelligence: Mapping Consensus in Ethical and Rights-based Approaches to Principles for AI." *Berkman Klein Center.*

https://cyber.harvard.edu/publication/2020/principled-ai.

HLEG. 2019. European Commission. "Ethics Guidelines for Trustworthy AI." https://ec.europa.eu/digital-single-market/en/news/ethics-guidelines-trustworthy-ai.

Benjamins, R, A. Barbado, and D. Sierra. 27 September 2019. "Responsible AI by Design in Practice." *Proceedings of the Human-Centered AI: Trustworthiness of AI Models & Data (HAI) track at AAAI Fall Symposium.* DC: AAAI. https://arxiv.org/abs/1909.12838v2.

O'Brian, T., S. Sweetman, N. Crampton and V. Veeraraghavan. 14 January 2020. "How Global Tech Companies can Champion Ethical AI." *World Economic Forum.* https://www.weforum.org/agenda/2020/01/tech-companies-ethics-responsible-ai-microsoft/.

Newmann Cussins, J. 2020. "Decision Points in AI Governance." https://cltc.berkeley.edu/wp-content/uploads/2020/05/Decision_Points_AI_Governance.pdf.

Benjamins, R. 2020. "Towards Organizational Guidelines for the Responsible Use of AI." https://ecai2020.eu/papers/1347_paper.pdf.

Benjamins, R. 6 October 2020. "A Choices Framework for the Responsible Use of AI." *AI and Ethics.* https://doi.org/10.1007/s43681-020-00012-5.

Wikipedia. n.d. "Cambridge Analytica." *Wikipedia.* https://en.wikipedia.org/wiki/Cambridge_Analytica.

Benjamins, R. and I. Salazar. 2020. *The Myth of the Algorithm: Tales and Truths of Artificial Intelligence (in Spanish).* Madrid: Anaya Multimedia.

Wikipedia. n.d. "Generative adversarial network." *Wikipedia.* https://en.wikipedia.org/wiki/Generative_adversarial_network.

Wikipedia. n.d. "Facebook–Cambridge Analytica data scandal." *Wikipedia.* https://en.wikipedia.org/wiki/Facebook%E2%80%93Cambridge_Analytica_data_scandal.

Wikipedia. n.d. "Social Credit System." *Wikipedia*. https://en.wikipedia.org/wiki/Social_Credit_System.

CHAPTER 20

Benjamins, R. 22 May 2020. "A New Organizational Role for Artificial Intelligence: The Responsible AI Champion." *Think Big Business*. https://business.blogthinkbig.com/a-new-organizational-role-for-artificial-intelligence-the-responsible-ai-champion/.

Benjamins et al. 2019. op. cit.

Fjeld, J., N. Achten, H. Hilligoss, A. Nagy, and M. Srikumar. 2020. "Principled Artificial Intelligence: Mapping Consensus in Ethical and Rights-based Approaches to Principles for AI." *DASH Harvard*. https://dash.harvard.edu/handle/1/42160420.

CHAPTER 21

United Nations. 2015. "Resolution Adopted by the General Assembly on 25 September 2015." https://www.un.org/ga/search/view_doc.asp?symbol=A/RES/70/1&Lang=E.

Expert Group on B2G Data Sharing. 2020. "Towards a European strategy on business-to-government data sharing for the public interest." *European Commission*. https://ec.europa.eu/newsroom/dae/document.cfm?doc_id=64954.

Verhulst, S.G., A. Zahuranec, A. Young, and M. Winowatan. 2 March 2020. "Wanted: Data Stewards: (Re-)Defining The Roles and Responsibilities of Data Stewards for an Age of Data Collaboration." *Govlab*. http://thegovlab.org/wanted-data-stewards-re-defining-the-roles-and-responsibilities-of-data-stewards-for-an-age-of-data-collaboration/.

World Bank. May 2020. "World Development Report 2021, Data for Better Lives." *World Bank*. https://consultations.worldbank.org/sites/default/files/consultations/16821/World-Development-Report-2021-Data-for-Better-Lives-Concept-Note.pdf.

World Bank. 2015. "Using Big Data for the Sustainable Development Goals." *UN Stats*. https://unstats.un.org/unsd/trade/events/2015/abudhabi/presentations/day3/02/2b%20A-Using%20Big%20Data%20for%20the%20Sustainable%20Development%20Goals%2010222015.pdf.

Pokhriyal, N., W. Dong, and V. Govindaraju. 10 June 2015. "Virtual Networks and Poverty Analysis in Senegal." *arXiv*. https://arxiv.org/abs/1506.03401.

Oliver, N. 5 September 2013. "Combating Global Epidemics with Big Mobile Data." *The Guardian.* https://www.theguardian.com/media-network/media-network-blog/2013/sep/05/combating-epidemics-big-mobile-data.

Lipsitch, M. 9 September 2009. "Use of Cumulative Incidence of Novel Influenza A/H1N1 in Foreign Travelers to Estimate Lower Bounds on Cumulative Incidence in Mexico." *PLOS ONE.* https://journals.plos.org/plosone/article?id=10.1371/journal.pone.0006895.

GSMA. 2018. op. cit.

Wesolowski A., Buckee C.O., Bengtsson L., Wetter E., Lu X. and Tatem A.J. 2014. "Commentary: Containing the Ebola Outbreak - the Potential and Challenge of Mobile Network Data." *PLOS CURRENTS.* https://www.ncbi.nlm.nih.gov/pmc/articles/PMC4205120/.

JRC. 2020. "Coronavirus: Mobility Data Provides Insights into Virus Spread and Containment to Help Inform Future Responses." *EU Science Hub.* https://ec.europa.eu/jrc/en/news/coronavirus-mobility-data-provides-insights-virus-spread-and-containment-help-inform-future.

Oliver, N., B. Lepri, H. Sterly, R. Lambiotte, S. Deletaille, M. De Nadai, E. Letouzé et al. 5 June 2020. "Mobile Phone Data for Informing Public Health Actions Across the COVID-19 Pandemic Life Cycle." *Science Advances,* 1-6. https://advances.sciencemag.org/content/6/23/eabc0764.

Santamaria, C., F. Sermi, S. Spyratos, S.M. Iacus, A. Annunziato, D. Tarchi and M. Vespe. December 2020. "Measuring the Impact of COVID-19 Confinement Measures on Human Mobility Using Mobile Positioning Data. A European Regional Analysis." *Safety Science,* 132.

ABOUT
THE AUTHOR

RICHARD BENJAMINS is Chief AI & Data Strategist at Telefónica. He was named one of the 100 most influential people in data-driven business (DataIQ 100, 2018). He is also co-founder and Vice President of the Spanish Observatory for Ethical and Social Impacts of AI (OdiseIA). He was Group Chief Data Officer at AXA, and before that spent a decade in big data and analytics executive positions at Telefónica. He is an expert to the European Parliament's AI Observatory (EPAIO), a frequent speaker at AI events, and strategic advisor to several start-ups. He was also a member of the European Commission's B2G data-sharing Expert Group and founder of Telefónica's Big Data for Social Good department. He holds a PhD in Cognitive Science, has published over 100 scientific articles, and is author of the (Spanish) book, *The Myth of the Algorithm: Tales and Truths of Artificial Intelligence*.